UNIVERSITY CASEBOOK SERIES®

CONGRESS AT WORK

A DOCUMENTARY SUPPLEMENT FOR COURSES IN LEGISLATION

PETER L. STRAUSS
Betts Professor of Law
Columbia University School of Law

FOUNDATION
PRESS

University Casebook Series is a trademark registered in the U.S. Patent and Trademark Office.

© 2016 LEG, Inc. d/b/a West Academic
    444 Cedar Street, Suite 700
    St. Paul, MN 55101
    1-877-888-1330

Printed in the United States of America

ISBN: 978-1-63460-638-7

In Memoriam
Arthur and Jack

and for the living
Joanna, Ben, Bethany, Noah and Lenox

WHY THIS SUPPLEMENT?

Casebooks on Legislation typically omit legislative materials, as such, and may present students with few opportunities to work directly with statutes and the process that creates them. They principally approach legislative work products through the eyes of judges required to decide subsequent litigation about their meaning—often years after passage, and in unusual contexts. Lawyers, on the other hand, may become intimately involved in the legislative process. Whether or not this is so, they often must advise clients about statutory meaning, in matters of great consequence, long before judicial readings occur, with only the statutes and any sense they may have about their origins to guide them. It is the purpose of this supplement to fill this gap. For two relatively compact statutes, enacted late in the 19th and 20th centuries, this supplement provides its users the primary materials of the legislative process and sets some associated problems for interpretation, with only enough context-setting text to frame the issues as clients might have asked contemporary lawyers for advice about them.

SUMMARY OF CONTENTS

TABLE OF CONTENTS

TABLE OF CASES

The principal cases are in bold type.

TABLE OF STATUTES

UNIVERSITY CASEBOOK SERIES®

CONGRESS AT WORK

A DOCUMENTARY SUPPLEMENT
FOR COURSES IN LEGISLATION

CHAPTER 1

RESPONDING TO ACCIDENTS INJURING RAILROAD WORKERS

BACKGROUND TO THE ENACTMENT OF THE FEDERAL RAILROAD SAFETY APPLIANCES ACT OF 1893

The Federal Railroad Safety Appliances Act of 1893 provides the setting for the first of these direct encounters with legislation and its materials. America's railroads were expanding rapidly in the second half of the Nineteenth Century, and an industrializing economy required them to haul heavier and heavier loads. Setting brakes by hand, car to car, and coupling them together manually was inefficient and increasingly unsafe.

PRESIDENTIAL COMMUNICATIONS TO CONGRESS

President Benjamin Harrison sent three messages to Congress urging it to enact railroad safety appliance legislation. The last was as follows:

December 9, 1891

To the Senate and House of Representatives:

I have twice before urgently called the attention of Congress to the necessity of legislation for the protection of the lives of railroad employees, but nothing has yet been done. During the year ending June 30, 1890, 369 brakemen were killed and 7,841 maimed while engaged in coupling cars. The total number of railroad employees killed during the year was 2,451 and the number injured 22,390. This is a cruel and largely a needless sacrifice. The Government is spending nearly $1,000,000 annually to save the lives of shipwrecked seamen; every steam vessel is rigidly inspected and required to adopt the most approved safety appliances. All this is good; but how shall we excuse the lack of interest and effort in behalf of this army of brave young men who in our land commerce are being sacrificed every year by the continued use of antiquated and dangerous appliances? A law requiring of every railroad engaged in interstate commerce the equipment each year of a given per cent of its freight cars with automatic couplers and air brakes would compel an agreement between the roads as to the kind of brakes and couplers to be used, and would very soon and very greatly reduce the present fearful death rate among railroad employees.

The industry was in fact developing automatic couplers and air brakes, but the variety of technologies on the market may even have increased the risk—forcing brakemen to deal with unfamiliar and potentially incompatible equipment that might trap them between two cars. And the common law offered little prospect for relief. Writing in 1893, the year Congress enacted the Federal Railroad Safety Appliances Act of 1893, Kohn v. McNulta, 147 U.S. 238, invoked "assumption of the risk" to deny recovery to a railroad yard switchman who had lost an arm in coupling two unfamiliar and incompatible cars two and one half months after starting work. "The intervenor was no boy, placed by the employer in a position of undisclosed danger, but a mature man [of 26], doing the ordinary work which he had engaged to do, and whose risks were obvious to anyone."

The next four pages set out the whole text of the statute, and three problems with which the lawyers for a railroad company might have had to deal. Excerpts from the debates follow, and also some excerpts from reports of the Interstate Commerce Commission, that had been made responsible for its implementation. What possibilities do you find in the statutory text? How should it be understood?

The Federal Railroad Safety Appliances Act of 1893

27 Stat. 531.

Chap. 196.—An act to promote the safety of employees and travelers upon railroads by compelling common carriers engaged in interstate commerce to equip their cars with automatic couplers and continuous brakes and their locomotives with driving-wheel brakes, and for other purposes.

Be it enacted by the Senate and House of Representatives of the United States of America in Congress assembled,

Sec. 1.   That from and after the first day of January, eighteen hundred and ninety-eight, it shall be unlawful for any common carrier engaged in interstate commerce by railroad to use on its line any locomotive engine in moving interstate traffic not equipped with a power driving-wheel brake and appliances for operating the train-brake system, or to run any train in such traffic after said date that has not a sufficient number of cars in it so equipped with power or train brakes that the engineer on the locomotive drawing such train can control its speed without requiring brakemen to use the common hand brake for that purpose.

Sec. 2.   That on and after the first day of January, eighteen hundred and ninety-eight, it shall be unlawful for any such common carrier to haul or permit to be hauled or used on its line any car used in moving interstate traffic not equipped with couplers coupling automatically by impact, and which can be uncoupled without the necessity of men going between the ends of the cars.

Sec. 3.   That when any person, firm, company, or corporation engaged in interstate commerce by railroad shall have equipped a sufficient number of its cars so as to comply with the provisions of section one of this act, it may lawfully refuse to receive from connecting lines of road or shippers any cars not equipped sufficiently, in accordance with the first section of this act, with such power or train brakes as will work and readily interchange with the brakes in use on its own cars, as required by this act.

Sec. 4.   That from and after the first day of July, eighteen hundred and ninety-five, until otherwise ordered by the Interstate Commerce Commission, it shall be unlawful for any railroad company to use any car in interstate commerce that is not provided with secure grab irons or handholds in the ends and sides of each car for greater security to men in coupling and uncoupling cars.

Sec. 5.   That within ninety days from the passage of this act the American Railway Association is authorized hereby to designate to the Interstate Commerce Commission the standard height of drawbars for freight cars, measured perpendicular from the level of the tops of the rails to the centers of the drawbars, for each of the several gauges of railroads in use in the United States, and shall fix a maximum variation from such standard height to be allowed between the drawbars of empty and loaded cars. Upon their determination being certified to the Interstate Commerce Commission, said Commission shall at once give notice of the standard fixed upon to all common carriers, owners, or lessees engaged in interstate commerce in the United States by such means as the Commission may deem proper. But should said association fail to determine a standard as above provided, it shall be the duty of the Interstate Commerce Commission to do so, before July first, eighteen hundred and ninety-four, and immediately to give notice thereof as aforesaid. And after July first, eighteen hundred and ninety-five, no cars, either loaded or unloaded, shall be used in interstate traffic which do not comply, with the standard above provided for.

Sec. 6.   That any such common carrier using any locomotive engine, running any train, or hauling or permitting to be hauled or used on its line any car in violation of any of the provisions of this act, shall be liable to a penalty of one hundred dollars for each and every such violation, to be recovered in a suit or suits to be brought by the United States district attorney in the district court of the United States having jurisdiction in the locality where such violation shall have been committed, and it shall be the duty of such district attorney to bring such suits upon duly verified information being lodged with him of such violation having occurred. And it shall also be the duty of the Interstate Commerce Commission to lodge with the proper district attorneys information of any such violations as may come to its knowledge: *Provided,* that nothing in this act contained shall apply to trains composed of four-wheel cars or to locomotives used in hauling such trains.

Sec. 7.   That the Interstate Commerce Commission may from time to time upon full hearing and for good cause extend the period within which any common carrier shall comply with the provisions of this act.

Sec. 8.   That any employee of any such common carrier who may be injured by any locomotive, car, or train in use contrary to the provision of this act shall not be deemed thereby to have assumed the risk thereby occasioned, although continuing in the employment of such carrier after the unlawful use of such locomotive, car, or train had been brought to his knowledge.

Approved, March 2, 1893.

COUPLING MECHANISM

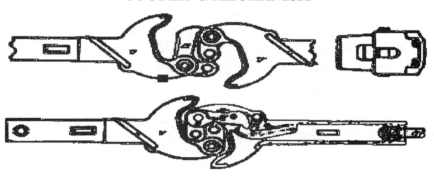

THREE SAFETY APPLIANCES ACT PROBLEMS

Outline your responses to the following problems just on the basis of the statutory text given above.

1.   Imagine yourself Southern Pacific's counsel in 1893. Your client's company has adopted the Miller Company's automatic coupler mechanism for its passenger cars, because of its valuable shock-absorbing qualities. For its freight cars, however, it uses couplers made by the Janney Company, which have proved more durable under abuse. The two types of couplers are automatic with others of the same type, but are incompatible with one another. The Company does not mix freight and passenger cars in the same trains, and since the Company's passenger and freight engines are equipped with the couplers appropriate for the cars used in their respective trains, the differences between Miller and Janney couplers will rarely present a compatibility problem in practice. Most of the large railroads have been making the same choice, with the result that freight cars are widely interchangeable among different roads, and so are passenger cars. When the two kinds of couplers are mixed, however—if, for example, a passenger engine must be used to move freight cars on a railroad siding, or vice versa—coupling will have to be done manually.

May your client plan to continue to use different couplers on its passenger cars than it uses on its freight cars? With what possible consequences and/or risks? What can you infer about statutory objective(s) and its/their bearing on this issue? What bases do you have for knowledge on issues of this character? What concrete steps might you take to resolve any issues of interpretation you find in the statute?

2.   It is now 1900, and you remain General Counsel to the Southern Pacific. Because your client is a "common carrier," as you well know, it has a legal obligation to accept cars coming to it from other railroads for transportation on its system at its usual rates, unless it has some legal justification for refusing to accept them. Wrongful refusal to accept cars could expose it to common law damage actions (as well as to a certain loss of commercial reputation). Has your client a legal basis for refusing to accept cars that will not couple automatically with its own

(a)   Because they entirely lack automatic couplers;

(b)   Because although they have automated couplers installed, they are Miller couplers, and thus will not work automatically with the Janney couplers that the Southern Pacific uses;

(c)   Because their Janney couplers, compatible with Southern Pacific couplers if they are in working order, are out of repair and so have to be coupled manually.

What consequences might your client face if it *accepts* such cars? What can you infer about statutory objective(s) and its/their bearing on this issue? What bases do you have for knowledge on issues of this character? What concrete steps might you take to resolve any issues of interpretation you find in the statute?

3.   The Southern Pacific Co. was operating passenger trains between San Francisco and Ogden, Utah. It habitually used a dining car in these trains. Such a car formed a part of a train between San Francisco and Ogden, Utah, where it would be ordinarily turned and put into a train returning to San Francisco. On August 5, 1900, the east-bound train was so late that it was not practicable to get the dining car into Ogden in time to place it in the next westbound train, and it was therefore left on a side track at Promontory, Utah, to be picked up by the west-bound train when it arrived. While it was standing on this track the conductor of an interstate freight train which arrived there was directed to take this dining car to a turntable, turn it, and place it back upon the side track so that it would be ready for the San Francisco train. The conductor instructed his crew to carry out this direction. The plaintiff, Johnson, the head brakeman, undertook to couple the freight engine to the dining car for the purpose of carrying out the conductor's order. The freight engine and the eight-wheel dining car involved were the property of defendant railroad company. The freight engine, regularly used in interstate hauling of standard eight-wheel freight cars, was equipped with a Janney coupler, which would couple automatically with another Janney coupler, and the dining car was provided with a Miller automatic hook; but the Miller hook would not couple automatically with the Janney coupler. (Because of differing orientations, the two could not "shake hands" in the manner suggested by the illustration above). Johnson knew this, and undertook to make the coupling by means of a link and pin. He knew that it was a difficult coupling to make, and that it was necessary to go between the engine and the car to accomplish it, and that it was dangerous to do so. Nevertheless, he went in between the engine and the car without objection or protest and tried three times to make the coupling. He failed twice; the third time his hand was caught and crushed so that it became necessary to amputate his hand above the wrist.

If Johnson now sues Southern Pacific for damages, what result? Is Southern Pacific in violation of the statute? Must/may brakeman Johnson be said to have assumed the risk involved in coupling the dining car and locomotive?

LEGISLATIVE BACKGROUND TO THE FEDERAL RAILROAD SAFETY APPLIANCES ACT OF 1893

To give you a lawyer's experience in assessing possibly relevant materials, the following materials have been edited less stringently than many you will encounter in law school. Read them with primary attention to what if anything they tell you about congressional understandings and purposes with regard to the interpretive problems you have identified. As you do so, you might want to keep track of

- Any differences between House and Senate approaches

- Changes that occur in the language of the proposed legislation as it progresses through the legislative process, and (to the extent you can say) what these changes were thought to accomplish.

- The genuineness (or not) of the debate—who is speaking, and what is his general position on the matter at issue; who is being addressed by the arguments made; your impression whether proposed amendments were well-intentioned or diversionary; etc.

52D CONGRESS	HOUSE OF REPRESENTATIVES	REPORT
1ST SESSION		No.1678

SAFETY OF RAILWAY EMPLOYEES AND THE TRAVELING PUBLIC

June 27, 1892.—Referred to the House Calendar and ordered to be printed.

Mr. JOHN J. O'NEILL, from the Committee on Interstate and Foreign Commerce, submitted the following

REPORT:

[To accompany H.R. 9350.]

The Committee on Interstate and Foreign Commerce, to whom were referred various bills to promote safety of railway employees and the traveling public, submits the accompanying bill in lieu thereof, and the following report:

ATTENTION FIRST CALLED TO SUBJECT.

At a meeting of the railroad commissioners of the country held at Washington in the spring of 1888, the reports from the States where railroads are required to report each and every accident showed such an extraordinary percentage of casualties to the men engaged in handling the trains that a resolution was unanimously adopted urging the Interstate Commerce Commission "to consider what could be done to prevent the loss of life and limb in coupling and uncoupling freight cars and in handling the brakes for such cars."

DEMAND OF EMPLOYEES FOR PROTECTION.

Following this railroad commissioners' conference the order of Brotherhood of Railroad Brakeman sent to the Interstate Commerce Commission a petition with 9,682 names attached, in which they ask the Commission to take such steps as they may think proper to bring about the adoption of automatic couplers and brakes on freight cars used on the railroads of the United States, and earnestly appealing to the Commission to urge upon Congress the necessity of national legislation, that the terrible slaughter of brakemen on the railroads of the country might be diminished.

As a result inquiries were instituted by the committee appointed by the National Convention of Railroad Commissioners and it was ascertained that during the year ending June 30, 1889, over 2,000 railroad employees were killed in the service and more than 20,000 injured. The publication of these facts awakened popular interest and formed a strong public opinion demanding legislation requiring the use of safety appliances.

* * *

NATURE OF ACCIDENTS.

We have carefully examined as to the nature of the accidents to which railway employees are exposed, and if the causes that result in so many deaths, so much pain, and such widespread suffering can not be mitigated if not obviated by legislation.

The demand of railway employees for the protection of the law came to us with great force as we recognized that they could not to any great extent guard against the casualties to which they were exposed; they must face the danger while others determined the conditions under which they labor.

The nature of the accidents to which railway men are exposed appear in the following tables obtained from the Interstate Commerce Commission:

Railway accidents to employees for the years ending June 30, 1889 and 1890.

Kind of Accident	1889		1890	
	Killed	Injured	Killed	Injured
Coupling and uncoupling	300	6,757	369	7,842
Falling from trains and engines	493	2,011	561	2,348
Overhead obstructions	65	296	89	343
Collisions	167	820	235	1,035
Derailments	125	655	150	720
Other train accidents	189	1,016	146	894
At highway crossings	24	45	22	32
At stations	70	699	98	691
Other causes	539	7,729	754	8,250
Unclassified	—	—	27	236
Total	1,972	20,028	2,451	22,396

The number of employees engaged directly in the handling of trains, June 30, 1890—that is, trainmen, switchmen, yardmen, engineers, firemen, and conductors—was 153,235, and out of this number there occurred 1,459 deaths and 13,172 injuries due to some form of railway accident. A glance at the above table for the same year indicates at once where the chief danger lies. The total number killed in coupling and uncoupling cars was 369, and the number injured was 7,841.

The number killed in falling from trains and engines was 561 and the number injured was 2,363; that is to say, 38 per cent of the total number of deaths and 46 per cent of the total number of injuries sustained by railway employees resulted while coupling cars or setting brakes, and whatever cuts off these two sources of great danger, would largely reduce the total losses of life and limb.

REMEDY SUGGESTED.

It is the judgment of this committee that all cars and locomotives should be equipped with automatic couplers, obviating the necessity of the men going between the cars, and continuous train brakes that can be operated from the locomotive and dispense with the use of men on the tops of the cars; that the locomotives should be provided with power driving-wheel brakes rendering them easy of control.

UNIFORMITY REQUIRED.

The efficiency of such devices, provided that all cars and locomotives be furnished with uniform type of coupler and brake, is generally admitted; without uniformity the danger to employees is fully as great as with the old link and pin coupler and hand brake, and representatives of the switchmen and trainmen who appeared before the committee stated that unless there could be uniformity they would prefer to go back entirely to the old link and pin; that the danger had increased from the use of so many different types, which statement seems corroborated by the large increase in casualties appearing in the statistics of 1890 over those of 1889.

STANDARD TYPE REQUIRED.

The interest of the railroads as well as the dictates of humanity demand that a standard type shall be established as soon as possible. The increased public interest in this question and the uncertainty as to what Congress may do has seriously retarded the work of fitting the trains with automatic couplers and brakes, which many of the railroads are anxious to apply, but do not deem it prudent to incur this vast expense with the danger of complete loss by the subsequent adoption, through Congressional action, of some different type.

With the standard type once established a large majority of the roads would take immediate steps to conform to it. Their managers are progressive, have an intense sympathy with their men, and from a strong sentiment of humanity, and also recognizing it as a feature of great economy to their roads, they would proceed at once to equip them with safety appliances, although it would require the application of a law to compel many of the roads to conform to it.

RAILROADS UNABLE TO DECIDE.

That the roads, no matter how well intentioned, by their own unaided efforts can obtain any uniformity of action on this subject within any reasonable time is not possible; they require the aid of law.

The secretary of the Interstate Commerce Commission last November issued a set of inquiries to presidents of different railroads.

The replies to the question regarding the best means of bringing about uniformity in safety car couplers are not clear in many cases, but the following statement shows as near as possible the position of the roads:

>   Roads representing 13,014.24 miles of road 69 operated—in favor of national legislation
>
>   Roads representing 46,791.09 miles of road 88 operated—in favor of voluntary action by the railroads
>
>   Roads representing 139.09 miles of road operated— 2 in favor of State legislation
>
>   Roads representing 11,915.88 miles of road 17 operated—in favor of the M.C.B. types of couplers
>
>   Roads representing 4,829.83 miles of road 10 operated—in favor of different couplers
>
>   Roads representing 9,447.79 miles of road 15 operated—expressing the opinion that the matter is still in the experimental stage
>
>   While 145 roads representing 38,985.59 miles of road operated—expressed no opinion
>
>   Several roads express themselves in favor of the Safford coupler

This report shows what might have been expected when taken in connection with the fact that there are forty-four different kinds of couplers and nine kinds of train brakes in actual use.

THE STATES UNABLE TO PROVIDE REMEDY.

The incompetency of the States to meet the situation is illustrated by the fact that the legislatures of Massachusetts, Iowa, Mississippi, Nebraska, Minnesota, New York, Ohio, Michigan, Wisconsin, and other States, realizing their inability to afford a remedy, have called upon Congress to act.

CONGRESS ALONE CAN ACT.

The national convention of railroad commissioners at each convention during the past three years have requested Congress to legislate upon this subject.

There are more than one million freight cars scattered all over the country that can be reached only by legislation of equal extent.

To obtain uniformity in couplers we must invoke the law of the United States to provide a method of securing the adoption of some standard type, and, if need be, to compel its use.

PROVISIONS OF THE BILL.

Five things appear to be fundamentally important, and for these the bill provides:

(1) *The application of driving-wheel brakes to locomotives.*—This concerns the safety of railway travel generally.

(2) *Train brakes for freight cars.*—The brakes have to be now largely operated by the brakemen, traveling over the tops of the cars by night and by day, through sleet and rain, exposed to great danger of falling from the cars or from overhead obstruction.

But with the train brake that can be immediately applied to the entire train the necessity of their going on top of the cars is obviated and a great measure of safety to all who travel will be brought into general use; for when the rails are in constant use by passenger and freight trains indiscriminately, running within a few minutes of each other, the driving brake and the train brake are essential means of safety to the traveler and the employee alike. No opposition has been heard to this requirement.

(3) *Automatic couplers.*—This has been previously fully discussed in this report.

The committee recognize that it is a serious question whether the best type of coupler has yet been devised, but they believe that if the railroads of the country are compelled to act, and reasonable time is given them to come together, the result will be the adoption of some uniform interchangeable type of coupler, and also train brake, that will prove satisfactory to them and will accomplish the result desired.

(4) *Uniform height of draw-bar.*—The railroads have themselves largely established a uniform height of drawbar from the rails with a maximum variation. It sometimes happens, however, that when cars are started out from the road to which they belong they do not get back for many months, and during that time the drawbars are getting down until they get away from the standard, in which condition it is impossible to couple them with those of a standard height without using crooked links, the difficulty of which adds largely to the danger and death rate. It is therefore considered highly important that a standard height of drawbar from the rails with a maximum variation should be maintained, and that cars should not be used when out of repair.

(5) *Hand holds.*—Until the changes contemplated by this bill can be affected[sic], and with a view to minimize the dangers by every means possible, we recommend a requirement of hand grabs or hand irons on all cars, something that the switchman or brakeman can seize to if he slips, instead of trying to clutch the side of a wet or perhaps icy car.

RAILROADS TO DESIGNATE STANDARD TYPE.

Believing that the standard type of coupler and brake should be established as soon as possible, it is provided that on July 1, 1893, the roads themselves shall by ballot decide, and in order to secure practical unanimity, that the vote of 75 per cent of the cars owned or controlled by the roads shall determine; and it is only in the event of their failure to agree then that the duty of selecting such type devolves upon the Interstate Commerce Commission.

WHEN LAW SHALL TAKE EFFECT.

In relation to the application of driving-wheel brakes to locomotives, most of them are now provided with them, undoubtedly within a brief time all locomotives will be provided with them, and it is only out of abundance of caution that the provision is inserted compelling their use after a certain date.

Concerning the application of safety couplers and train brakes, considering the enormous expense to the roads, we think reasonable time should be given.

The number of freight cars in use is 1,105,042, of which number about 87,390 are now provided with safety couplers and 100,990 with train brakes.

It is estimated that the cost of equipping a car with safety couplers and brakes is about $75 a car; which involves an expense to the roads of many millions of dollars. We provide that after July 1, 1895, all new cars, and all old cars sent to the shops for general repairs to one or both of its drawbars, shall be provided with the standard couplers and brakes.

The average life of a freight car is estimated at about eight years, and we think the provision requiring old cars to be fitted with safety couplers and brakes by July 1, 1898, is not unreasonable—believing also that the establishment of an outside date does not imply a delay until that time, as undoubtedly most of the roads would, as soon as the standard was established, provide the means and arrange for the change at once.

EXPENSE AND SAVING TO THE ROADS.

The expense seems enormous and would appear harsh and oppressive, but we believe in addition to the humane aspect of this subject, which touches all men alike, whether president, manager, or trainman, that the great saving to the roads in the cost of running their trains and in the loss from suits at law that they will be fully repaid, and within a few years.

EXPENSE TO EMPLOYEES.

In estimating the expense to the roads it is but just that some reference be made to the vast outlay of money by the employees in their voluntary relief societies rendered necessary by the refusal of the insurance companies to take the risk, which is due to the fact that death and injury is greater among trainmen than any other avocation followed by man.

The Brotherhood of Brakemen, to which but one-fifth of the brakemen belong, pays out not less than $37,000 per month—nearly half a million dollars a year. One order of the switchmen, numbering 10,000 members, pays out $170,000 per year. If all the different organizations of railway men would publish the amounts expended each year for the relief of their fellow-workmen, and the care of their widows and orphans, it would show in all probability an expenditure of several million dollars each year.

SAFETY TO TRAVELERS RECOGNIZED.

We recognize the extraordinary genius and enterprise of the railroad managers of our country, whose successful conduct of the interests in their charge is a marvel to the traveler, and to their wonderful management is undoubtedly due the comparative immunity from danger of the passengers on railways in the United States—during last year but one fatal accident to every 1,700,000 passengers carried, and but one injury for every 200,000 passengers carried.

The passenger trains, being provided with automatic couplers, the percentage of injury to brakemen in that branch of the service is very slight, and by comparison lends additional argument for the legislation we propose.

THE DUTY OF CONGRESS.

In conclusion it may well be considered whether any matter before Congress at this time demands, in justice to humanity and justice to the bread winners of the country, so much attention and consideration.

The railway employees of the country are in every sense among its best bone and sinew, splendid types of physical manhood and vigor. They are active, intelligent, strong, and brave men; in the flower of their youth, many of them with families. When we reflect that during this present year, judged by the statistics of the past, probably 25,000 of these men will be killed or injured, and when we contemplate the misery and suffering that will be brought to so many poor homes, the failure of Congress to legislate on this subject would be almost a crime.

APPALLING COMPARISONS.

To rivet the public mind on the appalling list of casualties and bring home to all men the frightful loss of life, a glance at some of the decisive battles of the world will suffice.

Wellington won Waterloo and Meade Gettysburg with a loss of 23,185 and 23,203, while the total loss on both sides at Shiloh in two days' murderous fighting was 24,000.

In the three years' war of the Crimea England lost in killed and wounded 21,035 men.

None of these terrible battles furnished a list of losses equal to the loss in a single year of our railroad men, a loss equal, in fact, to the entire present force of the United States Army.

In the Johnstown flood 2,280 persons perished, while during the year 1890 casualties on our railways resulted in railway employees killed 2,451 and injured, 22,394. The Johnstown disaster filled the imagination with horror and sent a thrill of sympathy throughout the civilized world, but that calamity came in one fell swoop, while fatalities on the railways, involving in the aggregate a far greater sacrifice of human life, have scarcely attracted public attention. Nightly several poor fellows are picked off—in the freight yard, on the rail—often the only vestige that morning reveals being a pool of blood and the dismembered remains of the unfortunate victim. Two lines of a newspaper headed "Brakeman killed," tells the whole story.

The vast army of maimed men, of homes left desolate, and of widows and children bereaved appeals to Congress for action.

CONCLUSION.

The committee desires to report the fact that it has been greatly aided in its investigations by the efficient secretary of the Interstate Commerce Commission, Edw. A. Moseley, whose experience gained from years of devotion to this reform and the data in his possession were invaluable aids to its investigation.

Also that through the courtesy of the general manager of the Baltimore and Ohio Railroad they were enabled to thoroughly investigate at the company's yards the merits of the present automatic couplers and brakes.

The representatives of many of the roads aided us to the fullest extent in furnishing information to enable us, if possible, to reach a solution of this question.

The committee recommend the passage of the bill and that H.R. 117, 180, 334, 582, 5134, 6187, 7512, 6648, and S. 2951 lie upon the table.

THE SENATE DEBATES (SOMEWHAT COMPRESSED)

24 Congressional Record (Senate)
Pp. 1246–51, 1273–77, 1279–82, 1284–85, 1287–88, 1323, 1330–33, 1370–72, 1375–76, 1416–18, 1423–25, 1478–83

February 6, 1893: Safety of Life on Railroads

[MR. CULLOM, Chair of the responsible Senate Committee, opened the debate by introducing the text of a bill in substitution for the one adopted by the House:]

SEC 1. That from and after the 1st day of January, 1895, it shall be unlawful for any common carrier engaged in interstate commerce by railroad to use on its line any locomotive engine in moving interstate traffic not equipped with a power driving-wheel brake and appliances for operating the train-brake system, or to run any train in such traffic after said date that has not a sufficient number of cars in it so equipped with power or train brakes that the engineer on the locomotive drawing such train can control its speed without requiring brakemen to use the common hand brake for that purpose.

SEC. 2. That on and after the 1st day of January, 1898, it shall be unlawful for any such common carrier to haul or permit to be hauled or used on its line any car used in moving interstate traffic not equipped with couplers uniform in type and action, coupling automatically by impact, and which can be uncoupled without the necessity of men going between the ends of the cars. And said uniform automatic coupler shall always be of the standard type established by such common carriers controlling 75 per cent of the cars used in such traffic. Said common carriers shall report to the Interstate Commerce Commission within one year from the date of the passage of this act the standard type of automatic couplers so established, but on failure to do so the said Commission shall designate and publish properly the type of couplers to be used.

SEC. 3. That when any person, firm, company, or corporation engaged in interstate commerce by railroad shall have equipped a sufficient number of its cars so as to comply with the provisions of section 1 of this act, it may lawfully refuse to receive from connecting lines of road or shippers any cars not equipped sufficiently, in accordance with the first section of this act, with such power or train brakes as will work and readily interchange with the brakes in use on its own cars, as required by this act.

SEC. 4. That from and after the 1st day of July, 1893, until otherwise ordered by the Interstate Commerce Commission, it shall be unlawful for any railroad company to use any car in interstate commerce that is not provided with secure grab irons or handholds in the ends and sides of each car for greater security to men in coupling and uncoupling cars.

SEC. 5. That within ninety days from the passage of this act the American Railway Association is authorized hereby to designate to the Interstate Commerce Commission the standard height of drawbars for freight cars, measured perpendicular from the level of the tops of the rails to the centers of the drawbars, and shall fix a maximum variation from such standard height to be allowed between the drawbars of empty and loaded cars. Upon their determination being certified to the Interstate Commerce Commission, said Commission shall at once give notice of the standard fixed upon to all common carriers, owners or lessees engaged in interstate commerce in the United States by such means as the Commission may deem proper, and thereafter all cars built or sent to the shops for general repairs shall be of that standard. But should said association fail to determine a standard as above provided, it shall be the duty of the Interstate to Commerce Commission to do so. And after July 1, 1893, no cars, either loaded or unloaded, shall be used in interstate traffic which do not comply with the standard above provided for.

SEC. 6. That any such common carrier using any locomotive engine, running any train, or hauling or permitting to be hauled or used on its line any car in violation of any of the provisions of this act, shall be liable to a penalty of $100 for each and every such violation, to be recovered in a suit or suits to be brought by the United States district attorney in the district court of the United States having jurisdiction in the locality where such violation shall have been committed; and it shall be the duty of such district attorney to bring such suits, upon duly verified information being lodged with him of such violation having occurred. And it shall also be the duty of the Interstate Commerce Commission to lodge with the proper district attorneys information of any such violations as may come to its knowledge.

SEC. 7. That the Interstate Commerce Commission may from time to time, upon full hearing and for good cause, extend the period within which any common carrier shall comply with the provisions of this act.

MR. CULLOM. . . . This or some other bill must be passed if there is to be any legislation at all on this subject, in pursuance of the calls upon us by the people, by the President, and by the two political parties. I may say well I remember very distinctly that the national Democratic convention censured the Senate for not having acted upon this subject before. I think under all the circumstances that there ought not to be further delay in the passage of some kind of a bill upon the question. Certainly the Senate committee has been disposed to be as kindly towards the railroads as it could afford to be and at the same time do anything in the direction of requiring these common carriers to put upon their cars and locomotives improved devices.

MR. GORMAN. . . . Mr. President, I never conceived when I gave my consent to legislation heretofore and aided in its passage that Congress would be called upon to regulate the running of railroads and the details of management, and to determine such questions for the hundreds of thousands of men who have invested their money in them, and whose genius and enterprise have made the railroads what they are to-day, to tell them by act of Congress what sort of engines they shall run, the kind of driving-wheels that shall be placed upon the engines, the length of the stroke of the piston, what kind of cars shall be used or what kind of a brake or coupler shall be used. . . . I am not prepared to put the railroads of this country into the hands of one man or five men appointed by the President of the United States, and confirmed by this Senate, who may be able to say to the great transportation interests, "You must spend $50,000,000 within the next five or ten years, or the next two years" . . . This Government was not constituted for such a purpose. It will be a failure when it attempts to say what shall be done in the modes of transportation and the character of cars that must be used.

There is an association of all the principal railroads called the American Railway Association of Master Car Builders, who have taken this subject up, and they hold a convention, I understand, at least once a year, with a view of determining what is a proper coupler to be used, and what other devices are proper to be used in the matter of transportation and in equipping trains. They have spent millions of dollars already in that direction.

It is true that there is no uniform device used by all the railroads. What is aimed at now in the proposed legislation is that there shall be a uniform device, and that that uniformity shall be secured at once by an act of Congress . . . I should doubt the wisdom of saying that Congress shall provide for a uniform coupler to be adopted by all the railroads themselves upon agreement, to be used upon all trains; but to follow it with a provision that if they fail to do it in one year the five or six commissioners who hold their sessions in the Sun Building, on F street, surrounded with a number of lawyers and clerks, well paid, . . . shall come to a conclusion as to what paraphernalia ought to be used in running the 40,000 or 50,000 miles of railroad in the country, it seems to me, is absurd.

MR. CULLOM. . . . So this subject has been before the Interstate Commerce Committee I think for three or four years, and from time to time we have heard gentlemen representing railroads and representing the employees of railroads and we have felt a degree of uncertainty heretofore (at least before the last session of Congress) in regard to the matter. . . . In the mean time the President of the United States has been calling upon Congress to act. In the mean time, as I said the other day, railroad commissioners of States have been calling upon us to act. In the mean time the labor organizations whose members have had the work to do in the conduct of the railroads have been calling upon us to act. . . . In the mean time the national conventions took up the subject. . . . Take the Republican platform adopted at Minneapolis:

> We favor efficient legislation by Congress to protect the life and limbs of employees of transportation companies engaged in carrying on interstate commerce, and recommend legislation by the respective states that will protect employees engaged in State commerce, in mining and manufacturing.

Then the Democratic convention at Chicago adopted the following:

> SEC. 19. We favor legislation by Congress and State Legislatures to protect the lives and limbs of railway employees and those of other hazardous transportation companies, and denounce the inactivity of the Republican party, and particularly the Republican Senate, for causing the defeat of measures beneficial and protective to this class of wage workers.

MR. KYLE. In regard to the suggestion made just a few minutes ago . . . that the measure is brought forward at the instigation of a number of patent holders, who wish to have these devices put into operation by the railroad companies, is it not true that the men who came to the great conventions of the Democratic and Republican parties, the persons who appeared before the committees there to get such a plank placed in the platforms, were the representatives of the great labor organizations of this country, persons who represented the railroad employees of the United States, who number thousands upon thousands?

MR. CULLOM. Unquestionably that is true. . . . [W]hile there may have been hundreds of gentlemen who sought to come before the committee with particular devices, the committee has always absolutely refused to hear anybody on the question of a particular device.

We have said to them, "We have nothing to do with your patents; we simply desire a uniform coupler that will be adopted by the common carriers of the whole country so that the laboring men engaged in the operation of the cars and trains shall be protected in their lives and limbs as far as possible when they undertake to couple cars together." . . .

MR. GEORGE . . . , [I]t is made the duty of common carriers to adopt as the standard type of automatic couplers that type which shall have been considered and adopted by a majority of the railroad companies in the United States engaged in interstate commerce. That is in section 2.

I should like to know by what authority Congress can confer upon the railroad companies of the United States, a majority of them, or any number of them less than the whole, the power to bind the minority in reference to a regulation of interstate commerce as defined in this bill. How is it, I should like the Senator to explain, that Congress can abdicate its power to make a rule regulating interstate commerce and leave that power to be exercised by an association of the railroad companies of the United States agreeing upon a certain thing? . . .

While I am up I wish to call the Senator's attention to another thing very much like the matter which I have read from section 2. I find in section 5 the following language:

> That within ninety days from the passage of this act the American Railway Association is authorized to designate to the Interstate Commerce Commission the standard height of draw bars for freight cars.

. . . I should like to know by what authority in passing a law regulating interstate commerce Congress can decline to exercise that power and confer it upon the American Railway Association?

MR. CULLOM. Mr. President, in the first place Congress has the power to regulate commerce among the States and with foreign nations, etc. Congress, as a body of men, can do nothing more than pass a law providing for the regulation of commerce among the States and with foreign nations, etc. In order to enforce a law for the regulation of commerce among the States somebody outside of Congress must exercise the power as the hand of Congress.

In the first place we passed a law for the regulation of commerce and provided for a Commission to stand as the representative of Congress. . . . The courts have decided that regulation of interstate commerce or interstate commerce itself not only applies to the articles transported from one State to another, but that the Government has the right to determine the vehicles in which this commerce shall be transported. . . .

I am myself unable to see any difference between the passage of a law providing for a commission to settle the question of what kind of device shall be put upon cars engaged in interstate commerce by the designation of some outside organization, if you please, who are experts, and who are not railroad owners by any means, but who are scientific men, and who can determine better what, in the interest of commerce and the protection of life and property, the device ought to be, than Congress itself or the Interstate Commerce Commission; I do not myself see any difference between the designation of that association who shall determine in some way what the devices shall be, and Congress itself determining the question, or the Commission which has been provided by the interstate commerce act.

Therefore, as the best means of arriving at what is the best legislation and the best devices for the protection of life and limb, the Congress of the United States proposes to designate this particular association. It simply authorizes them to do it. If they decline to do it, then we provide that the Interstate Commerce Commission shall do it, but the purpose of the Interstate Commerce Committee has been to keep as clear as possible, so far as Congress is concerned, of any responsibility for the selection of any particular device by its own vote or by its own examination of the several devices which have been made in the country. So I do not think, in all fairness, that the point made by the Senator from Mississippi is really a good one.

[In subsequent debates, Section 5 was amended to appear as on p. 3 above, but the reference to the Railroad Association was kept in.]

February 7, 1893: Safety of Life on Railroads

THE VICE-PRESIDENT. The Senate resumes the consideration of the unfinished business.

The Senate, as in Committee of the Whole, resumed the consideration of the bill (H.R. 9350). . . .

MR. CULLOM. Mr. President, I see that the pending bill is to have a tolerably hard road to travel in the Senate of the United States, but I am inclined to think that if we can ever get to a vote upon the question such a bill will receive the sanction of the Senate.

Now, as to the second section, that applies exclusively to what we call automatic couplers. An automatic coupler to equip a car costs about $25, while the power brake to equip a car, according to the testimony, costs from $45 to $75. . . . When we first began to investigate this question there were about 1,000,000, but now there are something over 1,100,000 freight cars in the country. The only provision in the bill in reference to what kind of a coupler shall be used, is that the roads themselves shall determine it by a vote or whatever means they may arrive at a determination, and when those controlling 75 per cent of the cars vote or report to the Commission that a certain coupler is adopted, then the Interstate Commerce Commission proclaims that fact, and that is the standard coupler.

The Committee on Interstate Commerce has been desirous all the time of avoiding all legislation that would look as though Congress was determining any specific type of coupler.

We have kept patent owners away from us. We have kept every one whoever it was away from us who desired that any specific patent should be adopted by the Congress of the United States. The committee thought that the scheme specified in the bill was as simple and as just and as fair a way to arrive at what the standard coupler should be as any other.

MR. HARRIS. In this exact connection I should like to ask my friend from Illinois if he is not satisfied by the testimony which has been given before his committee that the railroad companies of this country are adopting the automatic coupler, the self-coupler, as rapidly as in their financial condition they can afford to do. Such is my recollection of the testimony which has been given before the committee. . . .

MR. CULLOM. In response to the inquiry of the Senator from Tennessee, I will state that most of the railroads, and I might say all of them, insist that they are doing the best they can. I agree that they say that, but while they are saying that, not one-third of the freight cars of the country are equipped with these brakes or couplers. While that is true, and while the railroads are going forward at their own gait putting some on every year, the laboring men, the employees of the roads, the switchmen, the yardmen, the men upon the tops of the cars, are complaining that the roads are not putting them on as rapidly as they ought to be put on.

MR. VILAS. I should like to ask the Senator from Illinois, who has given a good deal of attention to this subject, if he has known any instance in which any of the railroad companies deferred paying dividends in order to add these facilities to protect the lives of their employees?

MR. CULLOM. I am obliged to the Senator from Wisconsin for asking me that question. The truth is, Mr. President, that while the railroad companies insist that they are doing the best they can, they are looking to their finances more than to the protection of life and the security to limb of the men operating their trains.

MR. HISCOCK. I wish to interject a question which is somewhat in response to the question asked by the Senator from Wisconsin [MR. VILAS] and also pertinent in view of the remarks which have been made. Is it not true that committees of mechanics connected with the railroad companies have absolutely failed in any such committee or conference—whether of three or five I do not know—to secure a majority, even, of any commission appointed in favor of any one device?

MR. CULLOM. . . . [I]t is true that there was more or less confusion or difference of judgment as expressed to the committee by the witnesses coming before us . . . [and] the men who had been giving the question attention differed as to the particular kind of bill that ought to be passed. So the switchmen, the engineers, and the yardmen all came before us, and some of them wanted one kind of legislation and some another. But all of them, I may say, wanted some legislation that would result in a uniform coupler, and in power brakes being placed upon the engines and cars for the protection of life.

Very few of them, if any, were willing to allow the situation to remain as it is, with one railroad putting on one kind of a coupler, another putting on another kind, and all of them going on at a slow pace, but all together doing something which resulted, as these employees used to say, in a degree of uncertainty as to the kind of cars with which they had to deal that caused a greater loss of life every year than the previous year.

The proposition was that if that situation was to continue they would rather go back to the old principle of the link and pin, and then when a switchman stepped behind a car, waiting for an engine to back up with another car to be attached to it, to couple them together, he would know with what he had to deal. But if he stood there in the dark, with his lamp in his hand, and an engine was backing up a train of cars to be coupled to the one he stood behind, not knowing what kind of a coupler was coming, he said the danger was greater because in that case he did not know what to expect. [T]he attempt on the part of the common carriers to put on different devices, slow as they have been in putting them on, has resulted in greater injury and a greater number of killed as a consequence of the confusion existing in reference to the coupling of cars, the fact being that the greater the number of improvements, until we reach a particular point of uniformity, the greater the confusion will be. But when the cars shall all be equipped with an improved coupler of a certain type, then the men engaged in coupling the cars will know with what they have to deal. . . .

The total number of railway employees June 30, 1890, was 749,301. The number killed during the year ended on that date was 2,451, and the number injured was 22,396. Of the above total of 749,301 employees, 153,235 were directly engaged in the train service, of whom 1,459 were killed and 13,172 injured. That is to say, out of every 105 men directly engaged in the handling of trains 1 was killed, and out of every 12 men so employed 1 was injured. In fact, it is proved by the statistics that the total loss in killed and injured in eight years is equal to the total number of men engaged in this service at any one time.

That seems to me to be a striking fact, if true, and one that ought to startle every man into the feeling, if he had it not before, that something should be attempted to be done to put an end to this indiscriminate slaughter.

MR. HUNTON. Mr. President, notwithstanding the very attractive, and even seductive, title to the bill, I have not been able to give my assent to its provisions. . . . [A]railroad life is one filled with hazards. A person who takes his seat in a railroad car as a passenger, or one who takes employment at the hands of a railroad company, knows that he is subject to disasters unavoidable in themselves, and the employee knows that he is engaged in a business which four times out of seven will ultimately result in his injury, notwithstanding all the efforts that can be made to prevent it. Notwithstanding all that has been said upon the subject, I believe the history of railroad employees will show that wherever there is a vacancy now in any position upon a railroad car or in railroad employment, there are from five to ten applications for that place.

I believe, for one, that a railroad, operated by men who have devoted their lives to the science of building and operating railroads, will be better conducted by the officers of that company than can possibly be done by the Congress of the United States, by the Interstate Commerce Commission, or by the American Railway Association, or even by a Democratic or Republican national convention assembled to nominate a President of the United States.

In the first place, a railroad company is bound to keep itself abreast of the improvements going on in railroading, and I understand, according to the decisions of courts on the subject, a railroad company that falls behind the march of improvement in railroad machinery and appliances is liable to anybody injured if that injury results from the failure of the company to have secured the very best machinery in the world that is known to the trade. So I say it is the duty, as well as to the interest of the railroad company, to adopt the best machinery, the best locomotives, the best couplers, and the best brakes, because the history of railroads throughout this land shows that if they fail to do so, and injury results to a passenger or employee on account of that failure, that company is held responsible for damages ensuing, which damages greatly exceed in the aggregate the cost of putting the improved machinery upon the railroad.

MR. WHITE.[1] . . . I think the Senator is far out of the way in his law. I think the courts have held that if the appliance is the one normally used, then the railroad company is only bound in that respect to ordinary diligence; that although the proof may be overwhelming that there existed better machinery than was used, that there were better appliances than were used, yet if the machinery and appliances which were used were those normally used, that justifies the railroad company and it is exempt on that account. If the Senator from Virginia has any law supporting the proposition which he states, I shall be glad to have him refer me to it.

MR. HUNTON. . . . I beg to call the attention of the Senate . . . that it has been proved before the Interstate Commerce Committee of the Senate, upon the testimony of an expert, that it would cost the railroad companies of this country . . . $75,000,000 to $100,000,000 to comply with this proposed law. . . . [T]he Southern railroads particularly have not the money to spend to go into the new equipment for in the pending bill. They have not the money to spend, and the question is if this bill passes, shall the railroads cease to carry passengers and to take into their employment laborers to run their trains, or shall they be allowed to carry on their railroads and perfect these arrangements and make these improvements as soon and as fast as they can? . . . I believe human life would be safer and the railroads would be run better for the preservation of human life if the management of the roads were left to the companies than if they were turned over to the American Railway Association or the Interstate Commerce Commission. For that reason, sir, I am opposed to the provisions of the pending bill.

MR. CHANDLER. . . . I am amazed when somebody has succeeded in so lengthening out and whittling down the provisions of the bill and then getting into it a provision that it may be utterly abrogated as to any railroad company which can convince the Interstate Commerce Commission that it ought to be abrogated as to that railroad company,

---

[1]   [Ed.] Edward White, Senator from Louisiana, became Associate Justice of the Supreme Court in 1894 and Chief Justice in 1910.

that then anybody should come here at this late day in the session, with the universal, popular demand there is for some legislation on this subject, and undertake by one means and another and by one suggestion and another to prevent the passage of a bill which, while it looks in the right direction, is not a bill, I am free to say, which the Congress of the United States owes it to the 750,000 railroad employees, owes it to the switchmen and the car couplers of the country to pass.

Just imagine what takes place every time a freight train is made up. A railroad employee, a laboring man, is asked to step inside the track, stand up against a car which is not moving, and watch the coming of another car, which is being pushed steadily up against the car near which he stands. It is being pushed up by the locomotive away at the farther end of the train, 100 cars off perhaps, the engineer utterly unable to see the space which is to be filled up by his train, pushing the train back, back, back, watching perhaps for a wave of the hand or a wave of a lantern to tell him when he has gone far enough. With that engineer moving that train this long distance off, there stands the railroad's employee waiting until the cars come up near to him, which a few inches nearer would destroy him. Then if the dead wood come together and his life is saved, he is to couple the cars.

I think it is a horrible custom; I think that the sooner it is done away with, whatever the expense may be to the railroad companies of this country, the better. It has been done away with as to passenger cars. We do not hear of any loss of life in coupling passenger cars. The killing of railroad men engaged in coupling passenger cars is entirely done away with, simply because the railroad companies of the country have put safety couplers on, and their workmen do not go in between the passenger cars to couple them. It is entirely done away with, while the horrible requirement exists as to freight cars.

MR. HAWLEY. Mr. President, I have been listening with some interest, and have summed up what seem to me are substantially the conclusions of those who are opposing the bill. In the first place, they say the railroad companies can do this work better than anybody else. They also allege that the railroad companies are doing it. Then I have heard another one arguing that they are not doing it because they do not know what to do. Another one says, you can not do much at it anyhow; railroading is a very dangerous business; and they proceed also to say substantially that they can better afford to let the killing go on because it will take $75,000,000 to prevent it. These reasons are slightly contradictory.

While I have great respect for the wisdom and power of the managers of the railroads of the country as a body, I do not believe them when they say the railroad companies can do this work better than anybody else. They say they will do it because they have a pecuniary interest in avoiding damage to property and in saving lives. So they have, and so has every citizen the highest possible interest in taking care of the sanitary condition of his own house, but the law does not trust him to do it.

The Senator from Virginia [MR. HUNTON] was arguing a little while ago that the railroads are more likely to do it because they have an interest in doing it. At the same time he can not be allowed to let the sewage of his house run all over his own land at random. He has got to obey the plumber. He can not be allowed to build a house just as he pleases, because he must take some precautions against fire.

When it comes to the question of contagious diseases you would suppose he would be sure to take a great deal of care, but the law does not trust him to do that; it does not trust him to take care of his own children; it does not trust him for fear there may be danger of contagion to the children around him. In fact, the thing known as government, whether it be a State or city government, does not trust any of you in the substantial things of your life.

MR. WHITE. Will the Senator from Connecticut allow me?

MR. HAWLEY. Certainly.

MR. WHITE. The report of the committee shows that for the year 1890 there was an increase of 94,787 cars in the United States, exclusive of those in the passenger service, and only 16,287 of them were equipped with train brakes, and only about one-third of those put in use during the year were fitted with automatic couplers.

MR. HAWLEY. I thank the Senator. I remember hearing the Senator from Illinois say the other day that somebody—I do not know who it was—had built 18,000 cars during the last year, and had made no provision upon them whatever in the nature of safety couplers.

I affirm that the railroad companies are not better adapted to take care of this matter than the Government. I say they will not do it and can not be trusted to do it, and they ought not to be trusted to do it. I say that without any disrespect whatever to anybody.

MR. WOLCOTT. . . . Mr. President, there is no question that a uniform coupler is a desirable thing. Any device which will minimize danger, any device which will minimize labor, any device which will quicken the transaction of the business of the railroads is desirable. We are all agreed upon that.

It is desirable that all railroads should have double tracks. There are infinitely more people killed by collisions on single-track railways every year than are killed coupling cars. It is most desirable that all over crossings to railroads should be built higher than they are or the roadbeds of railroads sunk lower than they are. It is desirable that substantial railings or other appliances be put around the tops of cars so that those engaged in walking upon them shall not fall off. More people are killed every year by falling off cars or by being pushed off by bridges than are killed by coupling cars.

It is most important that the danger at street crossings should be done away with. It is more dangerous to cross Pennsylvania Avenue at Ninth Street than it is to act as brakeman of a car between Washington and New York. It is most desirable that some measure should be passed that such crossings be elevated. There is danger in stairs. There is danger in steps. There is danger in almost every walk of life.

It is most desirable that so far as we can we should take measures to minimize danger to human life. We fixed upon railroads because it is so easy to legislate respecting other people's property. . . . In my opinion the man who is afraid to stand up and protect vested interests when they need protection, whether the substance of the proposed measure be included in party platforms or not, and whether the provisions appeal to the good sense of the different organizations of labor, federated or unfederated, is not fit to legislate for the American people.

Mr. President, there is not a railroad in the United States that pays a dividend or has paid a dividend for five years that has not adopted the most approved coupler which can be found.

MR. CULLOM. Will it interrupt the Senator if I make a statement at this point?

MR. WOLCOTT. Nothing interrupts me from the Senator from Illinois.

MR. CULLOM. I simply wish to state in connection with the remarks of the Senator from Colorado that the railways of the United States for the year ending June 30, 1890, received $23,367,873 from the Government for carrying the mails; and that for the year ending June 30, 1890, the railways of the United States paid in dividends on common stock $71,707,212, or 5.73 per cent, and they paid in dividends on preferred stock $15,364,401, or 4.42 per cent.

MR. WOLCOTT. I suppose to the average Grange audience to which the Senator from Illinois may be in the habit of appealing that statement carries some sense of conviction with it, but every man who knows anything about railroading knows that the dividends which have been paid on railroads to which the Senator refers are limited to the few trunk lines. Everybody knows that the great trunk lines of the country, the large railroad companies, are the companies which are prosperous, are the companies which pay these dividends, which seem to me quite reasonable. Everybody knows that the small branch lines, the feeders, the new roads in unsettled parts of the country, are, 90 per cent of them, without dividend earning power. Those are the roads which are to be affected if the bill becomes a law.

MR. WHITE. I do not want to interrupt the distinguished Senator in his very interesting and able argument, but—

MR. WOLCOTT. You do not.

MR. WHITE. I should like at sometime for my enlightenment as he goes on in his argument, if it does not disturb him, to notice one point. I find this difficulty in my mind. Taking all the statements which the distinguished Senator has made as accurate, how does that meet the difficulty that the railroads using their best endeavor at the present time, this best endeavor being used upon different roads, reach different conclusions upon different roads? Road A, using its best endeavor, reaches one conclusion and puts in one form of appliance; road B, using its best endeavor, puts in another form of appliance. If those two appliances brought together, because of their want of uniformity beget fatality to human life, does the argument of best endeavor remove that difficulty?

MR. WOLCOTT. No, it does not. The sum of the situation is simply as I shall state. There are five thousand patents. The vast majority of railroads in the United States say that a certain type which embraces some twenty-nine different patents is the best type yet invented and the type that should be adopted. Practically all the railroads—122,000 out of 170,000 miles—say we will try that, and as fast as we are able to do it we shall do it. They are spurred on by the awful penalty they pay for every employee they injure or every employee they kill.

Mr. President, this bill comes in under the guise of humanity. No man wants to stand up here and say that there is any sacrifice he would hesitate to make in the interest of human life. The destruction of life by coupling is tremendously overstated. The proportion of it that would continue to exist if we had the patent couplers is almost as great, in my opinion, as that which now exists.

You will find carelessness anywhere. You will find indifference to mutilation, indifference to pain, negligence the world over. These men realize the danger which they undertake when they enter the employment. They are not befooled. They know what awaits them when they enter upon their railroad job and they are paid proportionately. They get two or three times what they would receive upon the farm or in the store.

February 8, 1893

MR. PALMER. I should like to ask my colleague a question. I ask him whether it would not be entirely satisfactory to him to strike out all of section 2 from line 8 to line 15, inclusive. What is the object to be gained by retaining that provision? Why would it not be an improvement to strike out all that part of section 2?

THE SECRETARY. It is proposed to strike out all of section 2 from line 8 to line 15, inclusive, as follows:

And said uniform automatic coupler shall always be of the standard type established by such common carriers controlling 75 percent of the cars used in such traffic. Said common carriers shall report to the Interstate Commerce Commission within one year from the date of the passage of this act the standard type of automatic couplers so established, but on failure to do so the said Commission shall designate and publish properly the type of couplers to be used.

So as to make the section read:

> SEC. 2. That on and after the 1st day of January, 1898, it shall be unlawful for any such common carrier to haul or permit to be hauled or used on its line any car used in moving interstate traffic not equipped with couplers uniform in type and action, coupling automatically by impact, and which can be uncoupled without the necessity of men going between the ends of the cars.

MR. CULLOM. If my colleague will allow me to make a suggestion, I am inclined to think if those words were stricken out it would simply leave every railroad to have its own type of coupler and there would not be that uniformity all over the country which we are seeking. That might be the result of striking out the latter part of the section.

MR. PALMER. I may be allowed to say from my observation of couplers uniformity is desirable, and that there are a variety of couplers which may be safe, but on account of the ignorance of operatives their true office is misunderstood, and sometimes accidents happen, but if the law provides imperatively that the couplers shall be automatic and shall operate without the necessity of the manual interference of the individual brakeman, then the question of uniformity is entirely unimportant as the coupler acts automatically without the aid of individuals.

MR. CULLOM. It would be if the automatic coupler put on the cars of one railroad company acts in connection with any other automatic coupler put on the cars of another company, so that the cars will properly come together.

MR. PALMER. It is automatic in each instance.

MR. CULLOM. I confess I am not sure whether it would work right or not.

MR. HARRIS. I should be glad to ask the two Senators from Illinois who is to decide upon the first automatic coupler with which all other automatic couplers are to act?

MR. PALMER. If my colleague will permit me to answer, I will say that there is no necessity for any answer to be given to it at all. The requirement is that the coupler shall be automatic, that it shall couple and uncouple without the necessity of men going between the cars for that purpose; and if that end is accomplished, a certain type is a matter of no consequence whatever.

MR. HARRIS. There must be, if the Senator will allow me, a beginning; there must be some one coupler with which other couplers will couple, and somebody must determine what that coupler shall be.

MR. PALMER. Mr. President, the law imposes upon the carrier the duty of providing couplers of the character indicated in the bill. If he fails to do so, he is subjected to the penalties imposed by the bill. The question is not to be determined in advance, but the carrier is to be punished if he fails to comply with the law. What is the necessity for a preliminary judgment? The carrier has a plain, precise, specific duty imposed upon him, and, as in every instance where a positive duty is imposed upon a citizen, he must find the means of discharging that duty. No preliminary determination is necessary. The law requires that the couplers shall be automatic, that they shall couple and uncouple without the necessity of any switchman or brakeman going between the cars. It is at the peril of the carrier whether he complies with that law or not, and I propose to leave it just there, and punish those who disregard the law.

February 9, 1893

MR. BRICE. Do I understand that the chairman of the committee accepted the amendment of his colleague [MR. PALMER], striking out lines 8 to 15, inclusive, in section 2 on page 7?

MR. CULLOM. No, I did not accept it. When my colleague called attention to it, I stated that I was not sure but that it was a good amendment; but the more I have thought of it the more doubtful I am as to whether, if the rest of the section from line 8 is stricken out, the purposes of the section will be accomplished.

MR. BRICE. In that event I desire to offer an amendment, which I ask to have read.

THE VICE-PRESIDENT. The amendment to the substitute reported by the committee will be stated.

THE CHIEF CLERK. It is proposed to strike out section 2 and to insert in lieu thereof:

That on and after January 1, 1898, the use of any car equipped with couplers which require the person using or operating the same to go between or to place any portion of his body between the cars, be, and the same is, hereby prohibited.

MR. DOLPH. I suggest to the Senator from Ohio that his amendment, I think, needs a slight amendment. After the word "use" the words "by any such common carrier" are necessary to limit it to interstate commerce.

MR. BRICE. I accept the amendment.

THE VICE-PRESIDENT. The proposed modification will be stated.

THE CHIEF CLERK. So as to read:

That on and after January 1, 1898, the use by any such common carrier of any car, etc.

THE VICE-PRESIDENT. The question is on agreeing to the amendment of the Senator from Ohio [MR. BRICE] as modified.

MR. WHITE. I should like to ask the Senator from Ohio a question, if he will allow me. With the spirit of his amendment I think I am in sympathy. I wish to ask the Senator if under that amendment a car could not be run with the old vertical linkpin where a man would not be required to go in between the cars, and might use a stick? In other words, his amendment strikes out the provision in the bill providing for coupling by impact. I understand a man may possibly couple a car now by a stick, without putting his body between the cars.

Even with the old link pin, which I understand has sacrificed so many lives, it was not absolutely necessary for the man to use his body; and therefore, if my construction of the amendment be true, the amendment would leave the appliances just in the form in which they are now, and the statute it is proposed to enact would mean nothing.

MR. PALMER. It has occurred to me that if any alteration is to be made in the second section we should probably strike out lines 8 to 15, inclusive. The section would be in better shape with that portion stricken out than the proposition of the Senator from Ohio would make it.

MR. CULLOM. I was about to make the same remark. I think the proposition of my colleague made yesterday is preferable to the suggestion of amendment made by the Senator from Ohio.

MR. BRICE. That was the reason why I inquired if the chairman of the committee had accepted the amendment of his colleague. If he would accept that, I would withdraw the amendment I have offered.

MR. CULLOM. I have not accepted it. My own belief is that we should stand by the second section as it is; but if any amendment is to be made of the nature indicated I would prefer the adoption of the amendment proposed by my colleague to that of the Senator from Ohio. I suppose that my colleague intended to offer his amendment if he himself believes that it reaches the point desired.

MR. PALMER. If in order I will make the motion now that I indicated the other day, to strike out that portion of the second section, from line 8 to line 15, inclusive.

THE VICE-PRESIDENT. Does the Senator from Ohio withdraw his amendment?

MR. BRICE. I will withdraw my amendment for that purpose.

THE VICE-PRESIDENT. The amendment proposed by the Senator from Illinois [MR. PALMER] to the substitute of the committee will be stated.

THE CHIEF CLERK. On page 7, section 2, after the word "cars," at the end of line 7, strike out the remainder of the section, the words to be stricken out being as follows:

And said uniform automatic coupler shall always be of the standard type established by such common carriers controlling 75 percent of the cars used in such traffic. Said common carriers shall report to the Interstate Commerce Commission within one year from the date of the passage of this act the standard type of automatic couplers so established, but on failure to do so the said Commission shall designate and publish properly the type of couplers to be used.

MR. HOAR. I should like to call the attention of the Senator from Illinois [MR. PALMER] to the condition in which the section would be left if his amendment should prevail. It would then read, ending at the end of the seventh line:

> That on and after the 1st day of January, 1898, it shall be unlawful for any such common carrier to haul or permit to be hauled or used on its line any car used in moving interstate traffic not equipped with couplers uniform in type and action, coupling automatically by impact, and which can be uncoupled without the necessity of men going between the cars.

That taken literally I suppose would be nonsense, because it would only mean that the single car should have couplers uniform in style and action; but if, disregarding the letter of the section as it would be left, it means that all the cars used by any common carrier shall have couplers uniform in style and action with each other, and consequently to apply to all the cars that any carrier uses on its road, then there is no provision left in the bill by which the uniformity of the couplers put on the cars by one road with those put on its car by any other road shall be secured. Of course, as we all know, every train of freight cars consists of cars mixed up, coming by roads from all over the country. That must be the case. So the section, it seems to me, must require something more than would be left after the Senator's amendment should prevail.

MR. PALMER. The section would probably be quite as incomplete with the portions I propose to strike out as it would be after they are stricken out. But I would rely upon the third section as containing the cure of the difficulty, which provides—

> That when any person, firm, company, or corporation engages in interstate commerce by railroad shall have equipped a sufficient number of its cars so as to comply with the provisions of section 1 of this act, it may lawfully refuse to receive from connecting lines of roads or shippers any cars not equipped sufficiently, in accordance with the first section of this act, with such power or train brakes will work and readily interchange with the brakes in use on its own cars, as required by this act.

That would relieve one of the difficulties. I had supposed that after the very complete and thorough information and explanation of this whole subject given by the Senator from New Jersey [MR. MCPHERSON] to-day, in which he states the habits and customs and conditions of railway traffic in the country, no further detail would be necessary. The whole section as it stands, it will be understood, must be construed with reference to the general bill, and any want of precision in that particular section would be cured by the general and controlling intention of the whole bill.

MR. CHANDLER. The section in the bill as amended, if the motion of the Senator from Illinois is adopted, goes a certain way in the right direction, but it seems very clear to me that it does not go far enough. It is very evident that admitting it requires every common carrier engaged in interstate commerce to have automatic coupling cars, yet it does not require that those couplers shall couple with the couplers on the cars of other carriers engaged in interstate traffic. That will be the defect of the bill if it should stand amended on the motion of the Senator from Illinois [MR. PALMER], or as it would stand if amended by the amendment proposed by the Senator from Ohio [MR. BRICE]. It is then an injunction upon each carrier, but it is not an injunction upon the carriers altogether to agree upon a uniform type of coupler. Therefore, it seems to me that the bill would be very defective if the amendment is adopted.

If Senators will look at the bill as it was adopted in the House of Representatives, it will be seen that the House of Representatives thought quite an elaborate process was necessary in order to bring the various railroads of the country together. I refer to section 7, on page 3 of the bill as printed, where it is provided that every such common carrier shall file with the Interstate Commerce Commission the details of the couplers which are used upon the roads of that carrier, and when all the evidence is given before the Interstate Commerce Commission, then the Interstate Commerce Commission shall designate a standard type of coupler to which all the roads must conform.

It seems to me that some provision of this sort is necessary in order to bring all the carriers of the country into the adoption of a uniform type. While you seem to provide for an automatic coupler by requiring every carrier to have an automatic coupler, you have not reached the difficulty by providing that the automatic coupler of each company shall interlock with the automatic coupler of every other company.

Therefore I think the amendment of the Senator from Illinois and the amendment of the Senator from Ohio ought to be voted down, unless those Senators will annex to their amendments some provision by which we can bring the carriers of the country sooner or later to the adoption of a uniform type of coupler.

MR. BRICE. Will the Senator from Illinois allow me to answer the suggestion made by the Senator from Louisiana?

MR. CULLOM. Certainly.

MR. BRICE. I propose adding the following words to the amendment which I offered if it shall be renewed and come before the Senate, in order to cover the suggestion made by the Senator from Louisiana:

> That on and after January 1, 1898, the use of any car equipped with couplers which require or which in practice result in the persons using them or operating the same going between or placing the body between the cars shall be, and the same is hereby, prohibited.

MR. WHITE. I will state to the Senator from Ohio that my suggestion was not unfriendly to the purpose he has in view.

MR. CULLOM. As I was about to state, when my colleague made the suggestion of the amendment which he proposed yesterday, it occurred to me that it probably answered the purpose which we are all, or at least I imagine most of us, seeking, and that is to arrive at some system or uniformity of couplers which will result in the saving of life and the prevention of the injury which comes from going between the cars.

MR. BRICE. May I ask the Senator from Illinois a question?

MR. CULLOM. Certainly.

MR. BRICE. Does he consider the matter of uniformity a paramount consideration?

MR. CULLOM. I do not understand that there is any purpose to be attained by uniformity but that of safety to life and limb.

MR. BRICE. And if the purpose can be accomplished without uniformity, then it is not necessary.

MR. CULLOM. As far as I am concerned I am not wedded to any language or any specific provision in terms, if what is proposed accomplishes the purpose which I am anxious to secure and which I understood all members of the Senate desire.

The only trouble about my colleague's amendment, which occurred to me afterwards, was that one railroad might put on a coupler which would prevent killing and waive the necessity of going between the cars, but when it came to commingling with cars putting on some other device, perhaps a little different but general in principle, they might not come together in such way as to avoid the necessity of going between the cars and would not thereby protect human life.

MR. FAULKNER. Then, if the Senator will permit me, under those circumstances are they not prohibited by the bill up to the point where the amendment is suggested, because it is proposed to prohibit the employees from going between the cars if they do not couple by impact? Then under that amendment, if adopted, of course it would be a violation of the law, to go between the cars.

MR. CULLOM. All I desire to say further is that I am entirely willing to let the sense of the Senate be taken on the question of striking out the lines suggested by my colleague; and if the Senate thinks that that covers the case, that it protects these men, that is all I wish. If, however, I should come to the conclusion later on, after a more thorough and definite investigation of the question, or if in conference it should be determined that that is not sufficient, so far I am concerned I should try to remedy it. I am willing, however, without discussing the subject further to take the sense of the Senate on the amendment.

MR. HUNTON. What is the amendment of the Senator's colleague?

MR. CULLOM. The amendment proposed by my colleague is to strike out all after line 7, in the second section, down to and including line 15.

MR. BUTLER. I think we are all aiming at the same object, and I am quite sure the Senator from Illinois will conclude, after giving to it more thorough investigation, that striking out that part of the section will accomplish his purpose. If I thought it did not do so, I should not vote for it. I think, however, it simplifies the bill very much and really makes it more effective than by having that provision in it.

MR. CULLOM. As a matter of fact, I should prefer having the language remain as it stands in the substitute, because I wish to eliminate as far as possible any control over this subject by the Interstate Commerce Commission, provided we are sure of doing what we are trying to do.

THE VICE-PRESIDENT. The question is on the amendment submitted by the junior Senator from Illinois [MR. PALMER] to the amendment of the committee.

The amendment to the amendment was agreed to.

MR. GRAY. Mr. President, if I am in order, I should like to move an amendment in section 2, line 5, of the committee's amendment, that the words "uniform in type and action" be stricken out.

This seems to prescribe to the railroad companies engaged in interstate traffic, and which are to be regulated by this act, a uniformity in type and action of these automatic couplers, when such uniformity is absolutely unnecessary to accomplish the end, which I understand to be the only justifiable end of this legislation, and that is the protection of life and limb of the brakeman and those in the employ of the companies.

Leaving out those words, the section would read:

SEC. 2. That on and after the 1st day of January, 1898, it shall be unlawful for any such common carrier to haul or permit to be hauled or used on its line any car used in moving interstate traffic not equipped with couplers, coupling automatically by impact, and which can be uncoupled without the necessity of men going between the ends of cars.

I think we shall have accomplished by the amendment all that we may legitimately seek to accomplish, and shall not impose upon the railroad companies a condition which may have no reference at all to the end we have in view, but may very materially impair their ability to carry on the traffic which may be brought to their road.

For instance, suppose a railroad company receives every day, as all our great trunk lines are receiving, a lot of cars from another road, and though they may have the automatic couplers coupled by impact, which will not make necessary the interposition of the body of the brakeman to couple, they should not be uniform, what do we care whether they are uniform or not, if we accomplish the end that, in the language of this bill under my amendment, prescribes that they shall be automatic couplers, coupling by impact, and which shall not make necessary the interposition of the body of the brakeman?

Suppose a road, from caprice, from one of those antagonisms which come from the fierce competition for traffic, should refuse cars which come from another road, even though they may have an automatic coupler, one that will couple by impact, one that will not make necessary the interposition of the body of the brakeman, and say, "This train is not uniform in the character of the coupler, in type or action, and therefore we refuse to receive it."

I think that every extraneous and unnecessary condition should be eliminated from this bill, and that only those provisions should remain which are necessary to accomplish the great and humane end which this bill unquestionably has in view; that is, the protection of the life and limb of the brakemen on the railroads.

THE PRESIDING OFFICER. The amendment of the Senator from Delaware to the amendment of the committee will be stated.

THE SECRETARY. In section 2, line 5, after the word "couplers," it is proposed to strike out "uniform in type and action;" so as to read:

> That on and after the 1st day of January, 1898, it shall be unlawful for any such common carrier to haul or permit to be hauled or used on its line any car used in moving interstate traffic not equipped with couplers coupling automatically by impact, and which can be uncoupled without the necessity of men going between the ends of the cars.

THE PRESIDING OFFICER. The question is on the amendment to the amendment.

The amendment to the amendment was agreed to.

February 10, 1893: Safety of Life on Railroads

MR. MCPHERSON. . . . I move, in section 2, on page 7 of the copy of the bill that I have before me, to strike out the following words, beginning with the word "coupling," in line 5, to and including the word "and," in line 6; so as to make the section read:

> That on and after the 1st day of January, 1898, it shall be unlawful for any such common carrier to haul or permit to be hauled or used on its line any car used in moving interstate traffic not equipped with couplers which can be uncoupled without the necessity of men going between the ends of the cars.

The amendment eliminates from the bill anything and everything which directs railroads to put on car couplers which must be automatically coupled by impact.

The words in line 5, "uniform in type and action," I understand have already been stricken out of the bill. Now, if there is any reason for striking those words out there is equally a good reason for striking out the other words to which I have referred. This leaves the section then as I have read it. It directs the railroad company to have some form of coupler that will not compel the men to go between the ends of the cars to couple them, and without directing whether they shall use an automatic coupler which couples by impact or what it shall be. This amendment, I think, should be made.

THE PRESIDING OFFICER. The amendment will be stated.

THE CHIEF CLERK. On page 7, section 2, line 5, strike out the words "coupling automatically by impact and;" so as to make the section read:

> That on and after the 1st day of January, 1898, it shall be unlawful for any such common carrier to haul or permit to be hauled or used on its line any car used in moving interstate traffic not equipped with couplers which can be uncoupled without the necessity of men going between the ends of the cars.

MR. MCPHERSON. That is all you can accomplish by legislation, and I repeat it is infinitely safer, better, and wiser in every way, without any direction in a bill passed by Congress, to permit them to regulate their own coupling affairs in their own way, as will be most consistent with the public interest, because what is for the interest of the railroad in this respect is for the interest of the public.

MR. WHITE. Under the Senator's amendment will men be required to couple the cars without going between them?

MR. MCPHERSON. It does not matter whether the cars are to be coupled or uncoupled. The only thing we are trying to reach here by legislation is that the employee of the railway company shall not be required to expose his life and limb to the impact of the car. It may be done by a coupler which is adjustable by impact. It may by any other device which the railway company may seek to employ.

MR. WHITE. I did not make my question perhaps clear to the Senator. By the terms of his amendment will it be necessary that the cars shall be coupled without men being permitted to go between the cars?

MR. MCPHERSON. Most assuredly.

MR. WHITE. I ask that the amendment be read again.

THE PRESIDING OFFICER. The amendment will be again read.

THE CHIEF CLERK. On page 7, section 2, line 5, after the word "couplers," it is proposed to strike out the words "coupling automatically by impact and;" so as to make the section read:

> That on and after the 1st day of January, 1898, it shall be unlawful for any such common carrier to haul or permit to be hauled or used on its line, any car used in moving interstate traffic not equipped with couplers which can be uncoupled without the necessity of men going between the ends of the cars.

MR. MCPHERSON. It should read "which can be coupled or uncoupled." I will supply the words "coupled or." I did not notice that.

MR. WHITE. That answers my question.

MR. HOAR. . . . I understand that the old link and pin cars which are in use can not (sic) be coupled and uncoupled without going between the cars. A stick or some mechanism, four or five feet long, is used for the purpose, but practically the men will go between the cars. Practically they will be required to do so, for a brakeman who will not do it and takes the longer method, the longer time to do it, is very likely to be discharged by his company. So, as the Senator's amendment would leave the bill applicable only to cars which can not be uncoupled except by going within, we should have no practical legislation on the subject.

MR. MCPHERSON. We would have this legislation. The Senator speaks of what would be a practical working device. Certainly it has been proven by experience, and long experience, that the common cars now in use coupled with links can not be coupled and uncoupled in practice in any other way, except by going between the cars.

MR. HOAR. I understood the Senator to say just now that they could.

MR. MCPHERSON. I say they can not, as a practical fact, be coupled in any way except by going between the cars; and with my amendment to the bill, as I understand it, the effect of it would be to put on some devices that would not require the men to go in between the cars.

MR. HOAR. It is not true that the old-fashioned link-and-pin car can be coupled or uncoupled by a stick with a hook at the end of it without going between the cars?

MR. MCPHERSON. The Senator knows perfectly well that in the practice of running railroads in this or any other country such a thing would be totally impracticable and out of all reason.

MR. HOAR. That is precisely the point of my objection. The Senator has not described what can be done in practice under the bill as he leaves it. He has described what is possible. He uses the word "necessity." Therefore if the Pennsylvania or Baltimore and Ohio railroad shall go back to the old link and pin on every freight car, it has, as the Senator leaves the bill, a perfect defense to any legal complaint, because your bill does not say they shall not use cars which in practice forbid the men to go between, but you provide against cars where there is a necessity to go between.

MR. MCPHERSON. You require that they shall be coupled or uncoupled automatically by impact in the bill as it stands at present.

MR. HOAR. I am not speaking of the bill as it stands.

MR. MCPHERSON. Now, I do not care how they are coupled, if they are coupled by some device outside of the car by some system of leverage which may be employed, provided that it does not require the operator to go between the cars. I can imagine a device whereby an operator might stand on the outside of the car, by a system of leverage which is attached to the car. The idea, though, of directing the bolt or directing the link by a stick would be totally impracticable and to me very absurd.

MR. HOAR. On the contrary, several Senators have stated the reverse.

MR. BERRY. Will the Senator from New Jersey yield to me for a moment?

MR. MCPHERSON. I have promised to yield to the Senator from Ohio [MR. BRICE], and after that I will yield to the Senator from Arkansas.

MR. HOAR. Will the Senator pardon me one moment? The point of my question to the Senator is not in relation to the object or purpose of the measure. I am in accord with him as I understand him. I suppose, in regard to this matter, the Senator and I are exactly in accord in our desire as to what is to be done. The point of my question had reference to the mere question of phraseology. The Senator has offered an amendment, which, as I understand it, enables the carrier to defend himself if he can show that there is not an absolute physical necessity for the man to go in between the cars, although he still continues [to use] a form of coupler under which, in practice, every man will go in between cars. It is a question about the phraseology of the bill as left by the Senator's amendment.

MR. BRICE. It is precisely as to that point I wanted to make the suggestion that in the amendment I offered yesterday, at the suggestion of the Senator from Louisiana [MR. WHITE], I inserted the following words, which I will ask the Senator from New Jersey to incorporate in his amendment:

Which require or which in practice result in.

MR. HOAR. That is the point I want to get at.

MR. MCPHERSON. That I think would be a betterment. I do not know that the amendment I moved would be liable technically to the objection made by the Senator from Massachusetts. In practice it would not be at all liable to his objection.

THE PRESIDING OFFICER. The Senator from New Jersey will present the amendment in the form he and the Senator from Ohio have agreed upon.

MR. MCPHERSON. I move an amendment to section 2, which I send to the desk.

THE PRESIDING OFFICER. The amendment will be stated.

THE CHIEF CLERK. In Section 2, line 5, after the word "couplers," it is proposed to strike out "coupling automatically by impact, and which can be uncoupled without the necessity of men going between the ends of the cars," and insert "which can be coupled or uncoupled without requiring, or which in practice would result, in persons using them or operating the same, going between or placing the body between the cars;" so as to read:

> That on and after the first day of January, 1898, it shall be unlawful for any such common carrier to haul or permit to be hauled or used on its line any car used in moving interstate traffic not equipped with couplers which can be coupled or uncoupled without requiring or which in practice would result in persons using them or operating the same going between or passing the body between the cars.

MR. MCPHERSON. This answers, as I understand, the technical criticism made by the Senator from Illinois and the Senator from Massachusetts. I invite their attention to the phraseology of the amendment. My intention was simply to require the use of a car where the operative would not be required to expose himself to danger between the ends of the cars, and I think the phraseology will do that. I propose to leave to the railroad companies the adoption of such devices as they in their better judgment may see fit to adopt.

MR. CULLOM. It is very difficult to understand exactly what is couched in the language of an amendment offered in the Senate, and I hope the Senator will not insist on his amendment. Let the bill go through, and then I shall be very glad to consider the proposition as critically as possible with whatever light I can get from experts on the subject; and so far as I shall have anything to do with it, I shall endeavor in conference to arrange the matter properly.

MR. MCPHERSON. This amendment removes the objection which I have to this entire legislation, because you are attempting here to prescribe a certain kind of improvement which railroad companies must use, whether it is the best thing for them to adopt or not. If they can adopt any kind of a device which will prevent the loss of life by not requiring a brakeman or a man who couples cars to go between the trains, why not give them the opportunity of doing it?

MR. CULLOM. The amendment of the Senator would leave the amendment reported by the committee so that the coupling business may go on with sticks as heretofore. I want to call the attention of the Senator to the fact that common carriers now have rules by which the switchmen employed in coupling cars shall use these sticks or whatever they may be called. That rule is adopted, as I have understood, as a precaution against their being liable for damages in case a man happens to go between the cars and is injured. So I think the Senator had better allow the section to remain as it stands. I shall be very glad, so far as I am concerned, to change it later on, if it seems to me a safe thing to do.

MR. MCPHERSON. I do not wish to permit myself to neglect improving a bill as it ought to be improved in the Senate before it reaches a committee of conference.

MR. CULLOM. Let the vote be taken on the amendment, then.

MR. McPHERSON. Therefore I think a vote had better be taken on the amendment.

THE PRESIDING OFFICER. The question is on the amendment proposed by the Senator from New Jersey [MR. McPHERSON] to the amendment of the committee.

The amendment to the amendment was rejected.

MR. GEORGE . . . I wish to call the attention of the Senate to section 11 of the bill as it came from the other House, which the Interstate Commerce Committee have run their pen through and ask us to strike out, and have provided no substitute for it. I will say that the Senate will discover as soon as I do read it that without the eleventh section of the bill as it came from the other House there is but little if any protection to the employees. Now let us see what section 11 is, which the Interstate Commerce Committee ask us to strike out:

SEC. 11. That any employee of any such common carrier who may be injured by any locomotive, car, or train in use contrary to the provisions of this act shall not be deemed guilty of contributory negligence, although continuing in the employ of such carrier after habitual unlawful use of such locomotive, car, or train had been brought to his knowledge.

. . . [T]he Democratic House saw fit to insert a provision in the bill which would protect the employees. What does the Interstate Commerce Committee ask us to do? . . . The committee provide for a fine. What does that mean? It means you have to secure an indictment, you must have a grand jury, then you must have a trial before a petit jury, and then you must have a district attorney, and all that, and then the money is to go into the Federal Treasury.

When the poor man whose leg or whose arm has been destroyed, or his widow or personal representative in case his life is lost, complains, they are to be turned out of court upon what idea? That the employee knew that the railroad company whom he was serving had not complied with the law of Congress upon that subject. Is that fair? Is that just? . . . [B]y the striking out of the eleventh section of the bill they are denied redress.

February 11, 1893

MR. DOLPH. If no one desires at present to speak upon the bill, I wish to occupy a few minutes of the time of the Senate on an amendment which is not now before the Senate. But the Senate has agreed to vote at 4 o'clock on the bill. I understand it is the purpose of the Senator from Mississippi [MR. GEORGE] to offer the amendment, and if I wait until it is offered I may not have an opportunity to say what I wish to say in a few minutes upon the amendment. . . .

The experience of generations if not of centuries has led the courts and generally legislators to adopt certain rules in regard to the liability of an employer . . . that an employee who day after day works around a machine which is more or less defective and has knowledge of the defectiveness of the machine can not recover if he is injured on account of that defect. . . . The Senator from Mississippi proposes to abrogate this general rule in regard to common carriers engaged in interstate commerce, and to adopt a rule which, if applied to a housekeeper, for instance, would make the master of the house liable to his chambermaid if the cook left a pail of hot water exposed in the kitchen by which she was scalded, or which would make a corporation liable if two men were digging with picks in the same pit and one carelessly hit the other and injured him, notwithstanding both persons might have been employed with the utmost care and might have the best qualifications for the work. . . . [T]he rule which exempts the master from liability for an injury to a servant caused by the negligence of a fellow-servant and for injuries caused by defects in machinery which the servant is familiar with and has notice of is intended to secure attention and prevent negligence by an employee.

. . . The amendment of the Senator from Mississippi, as I understand it, . . . would abrogate the other rule which has been adopted by the courts, that where an employee works around dangerous machinery and continues in the employment when he might quit the employment, or when it was his duty to notify the master of the defect, he can not recover. Then it abrogates the other rule which has been adopted by courts, that an employer shall not be liable for injury to one servant by the negligence of another in the same employment.

THE VICE-PRESIDENT. The amendment will be stated.

THE SECRETARY. It is proposed to add the following as a new section:

SEC. 8.   That any employee of any such common carrier who may be injured by any locomotive, car, or train in use contrary to the provisions of this act shall not be deemed guilty of contributory negligence, although continuing in the employ of such carrier after habitual unlawful use of such locomotive, car, or train had been brought to his knowledge.

MR. WHITE. I do not understand that the doctrine of contributory negligence has any relation whatever to an employee continuing in the employment of his employer. . . . The doctrine of the bill that an employee is stopped from recovering from a corporation or from the employer, because of his continuing in the employment with a knowledge of the inadequacy of the implements used, does not involve the doctrine of contributory negligence at all. It involves another rule, which is an elementary principle, that the employee takes the risk of the employment. . . .

MR. WHITE. Let me read the section and call the attention of the Senator from Mississippi to it as I propose to modify it:

That any employee of any such common carrier who may be injured by any locomotive, car, or train in use contrary to the provisions of this act shall not be deemed thereby to have assumed the risk thereby occasioned, although continuing in the employ of such carrier after the habitual unlawful use of such locomotive, car, or train had been brought to his knowledge.

[Senator George accepted this substitute language, which thus became the proposal under debate.]

MR. GRAY. I think there is a very serious objection to this amendment, and I have doubt about the right of Congress, in regulating the instrumentalities of commerce, to stretch its powers so as to regulate the contracts in every respect which may be made with these people. I have enough doubt about it to control my vote.

Mr. President, this amendment seeks to introduce to every one of our forty-four States an amendment to the common law of that State of a character more far reaching than any which has ever been before attempted by Congress, so far as I can now recall, by one enactment. We undertake now to prescribe to the courts in every State in this Union a rule in regard to negligence, a rule in regard to the liability of employers, and a rule in regard to the ordinary risk assumed by all persons who engage with their eyes open in certain employment, to be administered not only by the courts of the United States, but by the courts of every State in this country, whether that contravenes the policy of a State or not, whether, in the opinion of its Courts or in the policy adopted by its Legislature, such a rule be wise or not. I believe that this exercise of power by Congress in this respect is unnecessary, and that there is no exigency demanding so far reaching and radical an exercise of power as would be made by this amendment if adopted.

The law in regard to the risks assumed by one man who takes employment from another are the product of a long series of years, of many decisions, of the philosophy of the best minds which have been devoted to the elucidation of that subject. They do not rest upon any capricious or haphazard foundation, they are not the result of hasty consideration; but they have been the development of the laws of human action and intercourse and relation of parties *inter se* which have been developed by our courts after argument and discussion through a long series of years and by many wise tribunals, with an entire consensus of opinion. I believe that it would be better to leave it so.

I believe that justice would be better administered, that the relations of man and man would be in a more satisfactory condition, if we were to restrain our hand, if we have the power—which I am not now discussing—from interference in this intimate and delicate relation. If the States choose to do it, that is one thing; they have the power; and in the competition going on between the States in the improvement of our jurisprudence, one State advancing tentatively and making experiments in this direction or that, and other States adopting it if they find that it stands the test of experience and the best judgment of the courts and of the public opinion of the country, I think that is the best way to attain these results, and the safest and surest way in which advancement can be made along these lines.

I do not think we have sufficiently considered how far we are invading the jurisprudence of the States, and how tremendous a thing it is if we reach out our hand and place it upon the courts of forty-four States in this Union, to control them in administering the law, which has been administered from time out of mind. I think there is no necessity for it and no exigency demanding our interference.

THE VICE-PRESIDENT. The question is on the amendment submitted by the Senator from Mississippi as modified. . . .

MR. CALL. I suggest to the Senator from Mississippi to strike out the word "habitual." It is entirely unnecessary.

MR. GEORGE. I will accept the amendment to strike out "habitual."

MR. PEFFER. I move to insert the word "the" before "unlawful."

MR. GEORGE. That is right.

MR. WHITE. I wish to make a very brief statement, if it be in order.

I entirely agree with the constitutional view expressed by the Senator from Delaware [MR. GRAY], but I do not think that constitutional view will operate to prevent me from voting for the amendment, because if there be a class of contracts which, under the Constitution, is not brought within the purview of this section by the operation of this proposed law and the Constitution upon which it rests, then this proposed law will not affect that class of contracts; but if there be a class of contracts which it is within our constitutional power to legislate in reference to, then I think the provision will be a wise one, and the legislation will be valid to the extent of its constitutionality, and necessarily invalid wherever it extends beyond the limits of the Constitution.

The Secretary proceeded to call the roll.

The result was announced—yeas 42, nays 7; as follows:

YEAS—42

Bate	Dubois	Kyle	Stewart
Berry	Felton	McMillan	Stockbridge
Blackburn	Frye	McPherson	Teller
Call	Gallinger	Mills	Turpie
Chandler	George	Morrill	Vance
Coke	Hansbrough	Peffer	Vilas
Cullom	Harris	Perkins	Voorhees
Daniel	Hawley	Proctor	Washburn

Davis	Hoar	Pugh	White
Dawes	Jones, Ark.	Sherman	
Dolph	Jones, Nev.	Squire	

NAYS—7

| Blodgett | Caffery | Gray | Sawyer |
| Brice | Camden | Morgan | |

NOT VOTING—38

Aldrich	Faulkner	Manderson	Sanders
Allen	Gibson	Mitchell	Shoup
Allison	Gordon	Paddock	Stanford
Butler	Gorman	Palmer	Vest
Cameron	Hale	Pasco	Walthall
Carey	Higgins	Pettigrew	Warren
Casey	Hill	Platt	Wilson
Cockrell	Hiscock	Power	Wolcott
Colquitt	Hunton	Quay	
Dixon	Irby	Ransom	

So the amendment to the amendment was agreed to.

THE VICE-PRESIDENT. The question now is on the amendment reported by the committee as amended.

The amendment of the committee as amended was agreed to.

The bill was reported to the Senate as amended, and the amendment was concurred in.

The amendment was ordered to be engrossed, and the bill to be read a third time.

MR. McPHERSON. I ask for the reading of the bill at length in order that the Senate may understand what amendments have been made.

THE VICE-PRESIDENT. The bill will be read the third time at length.

The Chief Clerk read the bill [whose language was by now nearly identical to the enacted statute] the third time. . . .

THE VICE-PRESIDENT. The question is, Shall the bill pass?

MR. BLODGETT. On that question I ask for the yeas and nays.

The yeas and nays were ordered, and the Secretary proceeded to call the roll.

* * *

The result was announced—yeas 39, nays 10, as follows:

YEAS—39

Allison	Dawes	Jones, Nev.	Pugh
Berry	Dolph	Kyle	Sherman
Caffery	Dubois	McMillan	Squire
Call	Felton	McPherson	Teller
Carey	Frye	Morrill	Turpie
Chandler	Gallinger	Palmer	Vilas
Cockrell	Gray	Pasco	Voorhees
Coke	Hansbrough	Peffer	Washburn
Cullom	Hawley	Perkins	White
Davis	Hoar	Proctor	

NAYS—10

Blodgett	George	Morgan	Vance
Brice	Gorman	Sawyer	
Daniel	Harris	Stewart	

NOT VOTING—38

Aldrich	Faulkner	Manderson	Shoup
Allen	Gibson	Mills	Stanford
Bate	Gordon	Mitchell	Stockbridge
Blackburn	Hale	Paddock	Vest
Butler	Higgins	Pettigrew	Walthall
Camden	Hill	Platt	Warren
Cameron	Hiscock	Power	Wilson
Casey	Hunton	Quay	Wolcott
Colquitt	Irby	Ransom	
Dixon	Jones, Ark.	Sanders	

So the bill was passed.

MR. CULLOM. I move that the Senate ask for a conference with the House of Representatives on the bill and amendments.

The motion was agreed to.

By unanimous consent, the Vice-President was authorized to appoint the conferees on the part of the Senate; and MR. CULLOM, MR. WILSON, and MR. HARRIS were appointed.

NOTES

(1) As the enacted text reflects, the Conference Committee accepted the Senate's changes on the matters of interest to us. Fairly read, what do the debates or other materials tell you about the purposes of this legislation? If you were describing the course of the legislation, how would you explain the changes that were made—for example, with respect to a possible purpose of securing uniformity of railroad practice?

(2) For each of the three problems on pp. 5–6 reconsider your initial response in light of the foregoing.

While these legislative materials may seem extensive, they in fact are rather condensed. The Senate debates alone fill 77 pages of the Congressional Record. Reflect not only on the light (if any) cast, but also on the propriety of consulting these materials or possible problems involved in doing so.

THE INTERSTATE COMMERCE COMMISSION PREPARES FOR THE ACT'S IMPLEMENTATION

The text of the Act and the debates implicate the Interstate Commerce Commission in the railroads' implementation of their new duties. The principal responsibilities of the ICC, a federal agency, were regulating the rates common carriers charged for shipments in interstate commerce, to prevent mistreatment of small shippers. Nonetheless, the Safety Appliances Act added safety regulation to its responsibilities. During the period between passage of the Act and the taking effect of its provisions, the ICC was called on to monitor progress toward compliance, to deal with requests for the extensions it was authorized to grant, and otherwise to act in ways that gave it both a view of implementation issues overall, and an opportunity to shape the railroads' understanding of and approach to the statute. Even apart from these responsibilities, it was an interested and well-informed witness to the railroads' efforts. Excerpts from a decade of its annual reports, 1893–1902, suggest both how the railroads responded and what were the principal problems of understanding or implementation they encountered.

These materials may be considered from at least three perspectives. The first and most straightforward is the perspective of interpretation. As you read these excerpts, consider the following questions

    1.   Would you have been reading them as they were produced, as general counsel to Southern Pacific? In what ways might you have sought to influence their content, or had the effect of doing so?

    2.   How does it appear that the railroads and/or the ICC understood the interpretive questions you discovered in your consideration of the three problems raised above.

    3.   What opportunities were there to resolve these issues in the ICC or using its offices, and to what extent were these employed?

    4.   What would be the risks, and what would be the benefits, of using materials like these in statutory interpretation, as indicators of statutory meaning?

Second, you might consider that we are now encountering a new kind of government institution with responsibilities for understanding and applying statutory commands, the administrative agency—one rare at the time, but very common today. In the late Nineteenth Century, statutes were relatively uncommon, shaping the possibilities for judicial action but leaving the courts in place as the principal resolvers of particular disputes. In the ICC we find for the first time a competitor to the courts, a mechanism quite distinct from the courts for the possible evolution of law, *and chosen by the legislature in preference to the courts*. The ICC's characteristics and possibilities for action are strikingly different from those of a court; its commissioners, appointed for only a limited term, are intimate with Congress and the regulated industry, self-starting, responsible on a continuing basis for policy implementation and, perhaps most important, have a variety of means available to them for action—conferences, the adoption of regulations, self-informing through inspections, the issuance of annual reports, the bringing of enforcement actions, etc.

Why might a legislature choose such a body? Might the resistance of the courts to changing established rules the public had come to regard as unjust—say. "assumption of the risk"?—play a role? What ought to be the response of a court, in dealing with questions of its authority, when the legislature does make such a choice?

Finally, these materials raise a question whether one should regard statutes as static texts, whose meaning is fixed at the moment of their enactment, or as more dynamic creations, susceptible as the common law is to change in response to emerging circumstances. The problem of *maintaining* railroad safety equipment emerged only with experience. Does it matter that the enacting Congress appears to have focused its attention on the initial stage of equipping cars with necessary appliances, if its language can be read to reach the problem of faulty maintenance as well? May agencies and/or courts properly adapt some/all statutes to problems that emerge with time, even if not foreseen or perhaps even foreseeable by the enacting Congress? The next pages will suggest to you that in the seven and one-half years between enactment and effectiveness, industry, worker and ICC understanding evolved through the processes of planning and interaction the Act created. If those developments might be relevant, it would be because we conceptualize the statute not as embodying a single transaction projecting a fixed meaning forward into the future, but as creating a constrained set of relationships that develop over time.

Like the legislative history materials set out in prior pages, these readings have been condensed, but not thoroughly pre-digested. They are presented in sufficient detail, your editor hopes, to provide you with a lawyer's experience of mining raw materials for your own sense of the possibly relevant.

The ICC's Seventh Annual Report, pp. 74–76 (1893): Safety Appliance Legislation

There was pending before Congress at the time the Commission transmitted its annual report for 1892, a bill entitled "An act to promote the safety of employees and travelers upon railroads by compelling common carriers engaged in interstate commerce to equip their cars with automatic couplers and continuous brakes and their locomotives with driving-wheel brakes, and for other purposes." This bill was passed, approved, and became a law March 2, 1893. . . .

In the exercise of the authority conferred by this act the American Railway Association on the 12th day of April, 1893, designated the standard height of drawbar for standard-gauge railroads at 34 ½ inches, measured perpendicularly from the level of the tops of the rails to the center of the drawbars, and the maximum variation at 3 inches. . . .

Communications from the leading railroads of the country show that the requirements of the law establishing the uniform height of drawbar has met with prompt acquiescence. . . .

For a considerable portion of the time necessary to effect the changes in equipment required by the law, a reduction of the number of casualties to railway employees, especially those which result from coupling cars, can hardly be hoped for. Experience has shown that dangers incurred in coupling cars are likely to continue while new devices are from time to time being introduced, owing to lack of uniformity.

It will be observed that the law does not in any way restrict the use of automatic couplers to any particular type or types, and therefore it can hardly be open to the objection urged against it that it would especially benefit a particular patentee.

In the matter of couplers the aim of the law is that the men shall not be required to go between cars in order to couple or uncouple them, and therefore a road must not only equip its freight cars with couplers that are interchangeable, but can not use upon its line the cars of other roads which do not automatically couple with their own. . . .

Tenth Annual Report 93–94 (1896): Safety Appliances on Railway Equipment

Sections 1 and 2 of the safety-appliance act, approved March 2, 1893, will become effective on the 1st day of January, 1898. On April 9, 1896, the Commission issued an order to all common carriers engaged in interstate commerce, requesting them to state to what extent they had brought their equipment into conformity with the requirements of these sections prior to April 1, 1896. In compliance with this order, replies have been received from 1,690 companies. Of this number, 727 report that they own or operate 33,323 passenger cars, 1,217,064 freight cars, and 35,898 locomotives; and 963 roads, most of which are operated by other companies, have no equipment. As shown by these reports, 32,962 passenger cars, or 98.91 per cent, are fitted with train brakes; 32,331 passenger cars are equipped with automatic couplers, or 97.02 per cent of the total number; 16,454 of the passenger cars so equipped are fitted with couplers of the Miller type; 15,426 have the vertical plane or master car builders' type; . . . .

Of the 1,217,064 freight cars reported, 360,079 freight cars, or 29.58 per cent, are equipped with train brakes; 448,014 are equipped with master car builders' vertical plane automatic couplers; 2,082 are equipped with other types of automatic couplers; while 5,236 freight cars are equipped with automatic couplers the type of which is not given; 455,332, or 37.41 per cent,[2] of the total number of freight cars are equipped with automatic couplers. . . . Many of the couplers claimed to be automatic only couple automatically with those of the same pattern or type, and not with the couplers in more general use.

Equipment of cars with this class of couplers will apparently compel the owning carriers to confine their use to roads using similar types and to trains entirely composed of cars so equipped. It is also indicated by the figures given in the returns that the rate of progress toward compliance with the coupler feature of the law which obtained prior to April 1 must be greatly increased if the equipment of the roads is to be brought into conformity with this statute on January 1, 1898.

Eleventh Annual Report 127–131 (1897): Safety Appliances

About October 1, 1897, the Chicago and Alton Railroad Company filed a petition with the Commission asking for an extension of time under the seventh section of the act, and similar petitions were also received from other carriers. . . . These petitioning roads owned a total of 1,164,932 freight cars. Of these, 29 roads, owning 125,413 freight cars, reported that they would, on January 1, 1898, have all their cars equipped with the automatic coupler; 43 roads, owning 195,512 freight cars, more than 75 per cent and less than 100 per cent; 55 roads, owning 394,700 freight cars, more than 50 and less than 76 per cent; 48 roads, owning 240,716 freight cars, more than 25 and less than 51 per cent; 27 roads, owning 107,765 freight cars, more than 10 and less than 26 per cent; 20 roads, owning 74,901 freight cars, more than 1 and less than 11 percent; while 72 roads, owning 25,925 freight cars, had equipped none of them with automatic couplers.[3]

---

[2]   [Ed.] In 1894 the proportion had been 25%.

[3]   [Ed.] That is, compliance with the act on the initial effectiveness date was expected to be as follows:

Number of lines	Percent equipped	Average number of cars/line
29	100%	4,325
43	>75%	4,577
55	>50%	7,176
48	>25%	5,015
27	>10%	3,991
20	>01%	3,745
72	0%	360

More than half the railroads (167/294) had equipped half or less of their cars; bearing out some of the predictions made in the legislative history, the 127 lines in better than 50% compliance were also the most powerful—owning among themselves 715,625 cars, 61% of the total.

A full hearing was had upon these petitions on December 1 and days following. The carriers were very generally represented at this hearing and made whatever statements and arguments they desired. Various labor organizations were also represented, particularly those embracing trainmen and other railway employees, for whose benefit the law was largely enacted, and these representatives fully presented their views as to what should be done under the circumstances. Certain testimony was also taken under oath.

Some companies had fully complied with the law, while other companies had made no serious effort to do so. There were a few instances in which companies had done substantially nothing toward compliance, although they had regularly paid dividends since its enactment. Such carriers do not apparently deserve the same consideration as does one that has done everything that could be reasonably required. An examination of the act leads to the conclusion that it was originally intended that relief might be granted in some instances and not in others, and that, perhaps, no general relief should be given at all, but the situation as a whole seemed to render any such application of the law at the present time impossible. . . . It appeared from the statements upon this hearing that from 40 to 65 per cent of the car mileage in such traffic was by foreign cars which came to the various roads in the interchange of business. To refuse to extend the time to a particular carrier was, therefore, to forbid that carrier to haul either its own or any other car not properly equipped. The road which had fully equipped, so far as its own equipment went, required an extension of time just as much as its connecting road, which had, perhaps, made no substantial progress in its equipment. To have refused to extend the time at all would have been to withdraw entirely from the interstate commerce of the country about 40 per cent of the freight cars, which would have been at the present time a very serious inconvenience to the public itself. The Commission felt, therefore, that any extension which was made must be made to all petitioning carriers alike. . . . We accordingly granted to all petitioning carriers an extension of two years with respect to both the first and second sections.

The whole number of train men employed during the year ending June 30, 1896, was 162,873. Of that number 1,073 were killed and 15,936 injured. Of these, again, 157 were killed and 6,457 injured in coupling and uncoupling cars, while 373 were killed and 3,115 injured by falling from trains and engines. Of other railroad employees, 72 were killed and 2,000 injured in coupling and uncoupling cars, and 99 killed and 783 injured by falling from trains and engines.

These figures appealed strongly to us against any undue extension. . . .

Thirteenth Annual Report 51–53 (1899):
Safety Appliances

. . . In November of the present year, however, numerous petitions from carriers were filed asking for a further extension of this time, and these petitions were set for hearing at Washington on December 6, general notice being given to the public. . . . The carriers based their claim to further relief upon two grounds: First, that they had acted in good faith, having made great progress in the equipment of their cars and all the progress that, under the circumstances, could have been reasonably expected; second, that to refuse to extend the time and to put the law into effect on January 1, 1900, would result in the enforced withdrawal from interstate traffic of a large number of freight cars, to the great hardship both of the railways, which would thereby be compelled to refuse traffic, and of the shipping public, which would thereby be denied the facilities for moving its traffic.

It was also urged that the necessary material could not be obtained and that the roads could not get possession of their cars for the purpose of equipping them in less than one year.

As to the first position of the carriers, it may be said that the progress towards the required equipment has been constant, as shown by their semiannual reports. . . . On December 1, 1899, the returns made by the carriers which had been granted an extension showed that practically all of their locomotives and passenger cars were equipped and that 1,250,808 freight cars were owned, of which number 1,137,229 were equipped with automatic couplers, or 91 per cent, and that 763,644, or 61 per cent, were equipped with train brakes. Where the grades are comparatively level, and this comprises a large proportion of the trackage, it is understood that not more than 50 per cent of the cars in a given train need be fitted with air brakes to make it possible for the engineer to control the train from the locomotive.

The second position of the carriers was also in the main well taken, as the immediate withdrawal of all cars not equipped with automatic couplers for the purpose of fitting them with that device would seriously cripple many of the railroads and would greatly inconvenience the shipping public. The great volume of traffic which was and had been moving for some months made it extremely difficult for the railroads to find the necessary cars.

The Commission also found that, owing to the great demand for all sorts of iron manufactures, the material necessary to make the changes required by the statute had been hard to obtain for some time past.

The petitioners asked for one year. Representatives of the railway employees who appeared at the hearing practically united in conceding that some further extension of time ought to be granted, but expressed various opinions as to the length of the extension. It was evident to the Commission upon the showing made that some further extension should be given, and after full consideration it was determined to extend the time until August 1, 1900. . . .

An inspector detailed by the Commission has visited numerous freight yards during the past few weeks. It appears from his reports that with reference to those appliances which became obligatory two or three years ago—grab irons, hand holds, and standard height of drawbars—an almost ideal state of equipment exists. Practically no cars are now found which do not conform to the requirements of the law in respect of those appliances. On the other hand, the condition of cars which the owning carriers had reported as equipped with coupling devices was often found very defective, and in some instances so much so as to reflect discreditably upon the roads.

A very large number of cars have been found where the appliances for operating the couplers, especially the unlocking machinery, were so out of order and unworkable that, though the cars were actually provided with automatic couplers, they could not be uncoupled without the trainmen going between the cars, and in some cases being obliged to resort to mechanical assistance in order to get the cars apart. Such a coupler is not automatic in the sense contemplated by the law. Its use subjects the men to risks and dangers which are obviously greater than those which existed when the old link and pin coupler was employed.

Fourteenth Annual Report 77, 79–84 (1900): Safety Appliances

The making up and movement of trains will always be a very hazardous business, and death and injury thereby caused can not be wholly avoided. In this connection the Commission desires to invite attention to what was said in its last report to Congress, for the Commission believes it as necessary to inculcate care on the part of the men as it is for the railroads to keep their equipment in order. . . . To the end that every precaution may be taken and that no careless, or indifferent, ignorant, or selfish individual may be permitted to endanger his fellows, a system of public supervision should be maintained and a close inspection made of the rolling stock in service, so that no wear or breakage may go unnoticed and unremedied. It is not proposed that such public inspection shall in any respect interfere with the duties of the operating companies respecting repairs, but that the inspectors shall see that cars in use are equipped with safety appliances, and those appliances kept in the condition contemplated by the provisions of law intended to promote the safety of traveler and employee. Such inspection will require some expenditure of money—small, however, in comparison with the interests affected.

Recognizing that a law of this character can only be made effective by a system of supervision and inspection, Congress appropriated $15,000 at its last session to enable the Commission to keep informed regarding compliance with the safety-appliance act and to render its requirements effective. This sum is mainly expended in the employment of inspectors. . . . The inspections have served to give a general idea of the conditions existing, and this has been of great value. The inspectors' reports indicate that violations of the law consist chiefly in failure to keep the equipment up to the required standard, including automatic couplers which are operative and in such working order that the men need not go between the cars. . . . It is reported . . . that probably 20 per cent of the couplers now used become nonautomatic through failure to keep them in proper repair. While in such condition it is agreed that they are far more dangerous to the men employed in handling the cars than the old link and pin coupler. When an accident in coupling now occurs it is said there is more probability of its resulting fatally. Again, when it was known that the men had to go between the cars to couple or uncouple it is claimed that engineers exercised greater care than they do now with couplers in use which are supposed to work automatically. These considerations indicate the necessity for most careful attention to the condition and repair of the appliances provided.

When railway officials reach the point of requiring car inspectors to reject any car having defective couplers or other defective safety appliances, as they now do on account of imperfect running gear, the dangers of railway operation will be largely reduced. It is understood that the most common defects in couplers are disconnected pin chains and loose brackets. . . . No prosecutions under the act have yet been found necessary. In cases where we have found it necessary to call attention to defects in appliances or in their operation the railroad managers have so far readily complied with not only the letter but the spirit of the law, and have not been inclined to cavil about the application of the statute in doubtful cases.

Fifteenth Annual Report 63, 65–69, 77–78 (1901): Safety Appliances

The number of conductors, brakemen, switchmen, flagmen and watchmen, killed in coupling accidents in the year ending June 30, 1901, expressed by the ratio of the number killed to the total number employed, appears to have been less than in the year immediately preceding by about 35 per cent, and the number injured by about 52 per cent. This appears in the following table, which covers 70 per cent of the operated mileage of the country.

Table No. 1—*Accidents incurred in coupling
and uncoupling cars.*

Year ending June 30—	Employees on 87 roads		Number of trainmen* employed to 1—	
	Killed	Injured	Killed	Injured
1898	209	5,433	555	21
1899	196	5,281	592	22
1900	228	3,970	546	31
1901	161	2,082	837	65

* Ratio based on trainmen other than enginemen and firemen, and including switchmen, flagmen, and watchmen.

The smaller ratios for the later years, as compared with 1893, indicate the increased security to life and limb effected by the partial introduction of automatic couplers and power brakes, the use of hand holds and compliance with the law fixing a standard height for drawbars. All of these improvements were introduced gradually and produced good results in proportion to the number of cars properly equipped, except that in the transition period, when some cars had automatic couplers and some had not, the dangers encountered by the men were greatly increased by the increased diversity.

. . . The increase in the efficiency of the men, resulting from larger locomotives and improved methods, which was marked a year ago, is still more marked now. In 1893 the number of ton-miles to each trainman employed was 638,635; in 1899 it was 844,638; in 1900 it was 913,425.

. . . White v. The Chicago Great Western Railway Company, recently decided by the United States circuit court for the southern district of Iowa, . . . involved the application and construction of a statute of Iowa, one section of which is quite similar to the second section of the Federal statute under discussion. Each statute prohibits the use of any car not equipped with automatic couplers so they may be coupled or uncoupled without the necessity of a trainman going between the cars. The plaintiff, White, was injured while attempting to make a coupling between a car that was properly equipped, in accordance with the provisions of both the State and Federal law, and the tender of an engine that was not provided with automatic appliances, which necessitated the use of the old link and pin. The United States circuit court instructed the jury to return a verdict for the railroad company, on the ground that a locomotive tender was not a car within the meaning of the act.

As the State and Federal acts are substantially similar, that court would undoubtedly construe the Federal statute as not broad enough to require the locomotive and tender to be equipped with safety couplers. If that construction shall be upheld by the Supreme Court, the safety appliance act will be considerably impaired in its practical value. It is therefore recommended that section 2 of the act be amended so as to specifically include locomotives and tenders. Such an amendment is necessary to put the statute in accord with the approved practice of all the prominent railroads. The reports from the roads to this Commission show that railroad officials, recognizing the need of uniformity in couplers throughout the whole length of a train, or a series of trains, have made good progress in equipping their locomotives and tenders with automatic couplers, and have so far equipped more than 75 per cent of them with such couplers. While this action is highly commendable, it is still desirable to add this reasonable and useful amendment to the law, if for no other reason than to insure uniformity among all of the roads.

Sixteenth Annual Report 57–59, 61–63 (1902): The Safety Appliance Law

The gratifying results of the law of 1893, requiring the use of automatic car couplers and of power brakes, were spoken of in the Fifteenth Annual Report. The benefits of the law have been increasingly evident during the past year. In particular, the number of persons killed and injured in coupling and uncoupling cars during the year ending June 30, 1902—the first entire year reported since the law went into full effect—shows a diminution as compared with 1893, the year in which the law was passed, of 68 per cent in the number killed and 81 per cent in the number injured. . . . But casualties continue to occur, and their number is such as to call for continued and earnest efforts to eliminate their causes. . . .

The report of the chief inspector, which appears as an Appendix to this report, gives a mass of interesting data concerning the condition of couplers on the freight cars of the country. He shows that during the fiscal year ending June 30, 1902, the 10 inspectors employed by the Commission examined 161,371 cars, as compared with 98,624 examined by the smaller number of inspectors during the year before. The number of cars on which one or more defects were found was 42,718, as compared with 19,462; the percentage found defective was 26.47, as compared with 19.73. This condition is due, not to worse conditions, but to the more systematic inspection of air brakes, the inspections of the earlier year having been devoted more particularly to couplers. The principal features in which the condition of couplers shows improvement are the increased use of solid knuckles and a diminution in the number of uncoupling rods incorrectly applied. On the other hand, some of the unsatisfactory conditions are as bad as ever. The poor maintenance of locking pins, a vital part of every coupler, calls for criticism, the number of defects reported under this head being 559, as compared with 128 the previous year. Almost one fourth of the 559 cases were "wrong pin or block," a broken pin having been replaced by one not designed for that particular pattern of coupler.

In Johnson v. Southern Pacific Company (117 Fed. Rep., 462) the eighth United States circuit court of appeals held, in August last, that the equipment of a car with automatic couplers which will couple automatically with those of the same kind is compliance with the safety-appliance act of March 2, 1893, and that the act does not require cars used in interstate commerce to be equipped with couplers which will couple automatically with cars equipped with automatic couplers of other makes. If this ruling should be upheld on appeal it would have the effect of nullifying a main object of the statute, which is to secure such uniformity in applied automatic coupling devices as to permit all cars in a train to be coupled and uncoupled without requiring men to go between the cars. The act in terms prohibits any carrier from hauling or permitting to be "hauled or used on its line any car used in moving interstate traffic not equipped with couplers coupling automatically by impact, and which can be uncoupled without the necessity of men going between the ends of the cars." Carriers are left free by the statute to use any kind of automatic coupler they see fit, the sole and governing restriction being that, whatever kinds of coupler may be used, no cars shall be hauled or used on the line which do not couple automatically by impact, or can not be uncoupled without men going between the cars; and this applies to the hauling of all cars, whether owned by the carrier operating the road or by other carriers. Plainly, if carriers use different types of couplers which do not work automatically with each other, the law is violated when a carrier undertakes to haul two cars so equipped in the same train. This was pointed out by the Commission in its report to Congress for the year 1893, and has been generally understood and followed by carriers throughout the country.

That a remedial statute which has proved of such benefit to a large and important number of citizens should be rendered nugatory by a decision in a case brought by an individual to recover personal damages without the Government's representative being heard upon a proper construction of the statute is unfortunate, to say the least, and an effort will be made to have it properly presented.

NOTE

The facts of the third problem you have been considering were those underlying the just-mentioned Eighth Circuit decision in Johnson v. Southern Pacific Co., an accident occurring four days after the Federal Railway Safety Appliances Act finally took effect. Judge Sanborn's opinion, driven by allegiance to the common-law "assumption of the risk" defense and indifference to statutory purpose, was understandably used by Henry Hart and Albert Sacks in their influential teaching materials, The Legal Process, as an exemplar of the problems with "plain meaning" approaches to statutory interpretation. A government lawyer did appear before the Supreme Court when the case was taken to it on certiorari, and a unanimous opinion favoring brakeman Johnson resulted—relying for confirmation of its judgment about statutory purpose and meaning on the legislative history you have read. Johnson v. Southern Pacific Co., 196 U.S. 1 (1904). Three years later, Justice, formerly Senator Edward White would cast the deciding vote in an "automatic coupler" case involving, precisely, the difference between contributory negligence and assumption of the risk—the change he had caused in Section 8. Schlemmer v. Buffalo, Rochester & Pittsburg R. Co., 205 U.S. 1 (1907).

CHAPTER 2

HELPING PARENTS MEET THE COSTS OF SECURING SPECIAL EDUCATION FOR THEIR CHILD

The pages following concern statutory developments occurring in the course of an extended dialog between Congress and the Supreme Court over issues associated with the reimbursement of prevailing parties' litigation expenses. Litigation imposes costs on both sides, winning and losing, and on the public. The private costs each side incurs include hiring attorneys, compensating expert witnesses, conducting investigations, and the like. The cost of providing a forum for resolution of their dispute, perhaps substantial, is largely independent of their efforts and must be borne by the public unless some or all of it is allocated to one or both sides of the dispute. The question who should bear which of these costs has long been debated.

In England, the general solution has been that the losing party in litigation is obliged to reimburse both public costs *and* the victorious party for its reasonable costs. This is thought both to encourage defendants who expect to be found liable to settle before trial, and to discourage plaintiffs from bringing suit if their causes of action are weak. But the English rule also works to favor richer litigants (that is, those better able to absorb the other side's litigation costs should they lose) over poorer ones—in particular, it discourages litigation by poor victims.

American law eventually adopted as a general solution to the cost allocation question that each side would in general be responsible only for its own litigating expenses. This approach has operated together with the "contingency fee" (which permits attorneys to take cases on the basis of being paid a percentage of any recovery if their plaintiff clients prevail, but not otherwise) to permit poorer litigants—injured workers, for example—to secure representation they could not otherwise afford. The established bar frowned on the contingency fee as an invitation to excessive litigation (against their paying clients), but lost that battle. Under the "American rule," a losing party might or might not be assessed a defined category of "costs" reflecting some of the public costs of providing a forum (depending on the court's assessment of the merits of its claims or defenses); but it would be required to reimburse its opponent for the opponent's litigation expenses *only* if it could be found to have litigated in bad faith. Even with the contingency fee, richer and poorer were still in imbalance; by aggressive litigation tactics, the richer could impose expenses on its poorer opponent that the latter could find difficult to bear.[1] Yet for litigants using the courts in good faith, the American rule removed the overhanging threat of having to pay one's opponent's litigating costs on top of court costs. Since 1853, the general federal statutes respecting the assessment of "costs" in litigation have reflected this approach, subject to some statutory variation.

Would it be proper for courts, in advance of legislation, to develop an equitable exception to this general approach for plaintiffs successfully suing to protect or enforce public values? In a number of contexts, the Supreme Court had recognized the authority of federal courts to award attorney's fees to litigants who had been successful in obtaining the injunctive relief associated with the "equity" courts (chanceries), rather than the monetary remedies characteristic of the "common law" courts of English legal history. Thus, in HALL V. COLE, 412 U.S. 1 (U.S. 1973), an action seeking relief under Section 102 of the Labor-Management Reporting and Disclosure Act of 1959 (Act), 29 U.S.C.S. § 412, the Court awarded attorney's fees to a successful union plaintiff in the face of arguments that Congress had implicitly decided to stay with the American rule by providing for such awards in some circumstances, but not those before the Court.

> "Although the traditional American rule ordinarily disfavors the allowance of attorneys' fees in the absence of statutory or contractual authorization, federal courts, in the exercise of their equitable powers, may award attorneys' fees when the interests of justice so require. Indeed, the power to award such fees 'is part of the original authority of the chancellor to do equity in a particular situation,' Sprague v. Ticonic National Bank, 307 U.S. 161, 166 (1939), and federal courts do not hesitate to exercise this inherent equitable power whenever 'overriding considerations indicate the need for such a recovery.' Mills v. Electric Auto-Lite Co., 396 U.S. 375, 391–392 (1970); see Fleischmann Distilling Corp. v. Maier Brewing Co., 386 U.S. 714, 718 (1967). . . . [While] § 102 does not 'meticulously detail the remedies available to a plaintiff,' . . . we cannot fairly infer from the language of that provision an intent to deny to the courts the traditional equitable power to grant counsel fees in 'appropriate' situations."

Justices White and Rehnquist dissented in a very brief opinion asserting their wish for "a far clearer signal from Congress than we have here to permit awarding attorneys' fees in member-union litigation, which so often involves private feuding having no general significance." At 16.

This equitable exception to the American rule found increasing lower court recognition in "public interest" litigation seeking equitable, injunctive relief. In court orders offering relief from continuing racial

---

[1]   For a magnificently told example, in a contemporary context, read Jonathan Haar, A Civil Action (1995).

discrimination and from environmental harms, court orders directed
reimbursement for witness expenses as well as for legal fees. To obtain
such an order, a plaintiff had to demonstrate not only success, but also
that its claims had vindicated an important, general public interest as
"private attorney general." These cases awarding expenses on an
equitable basis did not distinguish among attorneys' fees and frequently
compensated other expenses such as expert witnesses. In BRADLEY V.
SCHOOL BOARD OF RICHMOND, 416 U.S. 696 (1974), the Supreme Court,
reversing the Fourth Circuit, upheld such an order in a school
desegregation case. The lower court had voiced fear of the consequences
of recognizing this exception to the American rule, even in desegregation
cases, given

> the difficult and complex task of determining what is public
> policy, an issue normally reserved for legislative determination,
> and, even more difficult, which public policy warrants the
> encouragement of award of fees to attorneys for private litigants
> who voluntarily take upon themselves the character of private
> attorneys-general. . . .   [W]hether   the   enforcement   of
> Congressional purpose in all these cases commands an award of
> attorney's fees is a matter for legislative determination. And
> Congress has not been reticent in expressing such purpose in
> those cases where it conceives that such special award is
> appropriate."

Bradley v. School Board, 472 F.2d 318, 329–30 (4th Cir. Va. 1972).

The Supreme Court's reversal in *Bradley* substantially relied on a
statute that has been enacted shortly before the Fourth Circuit's opinion
had been issued. Very soon afterwards, the Fourth Circuit's reasoning
found expression in ALYESKA PIPELINE SERVICE CO. V. WILDERNESS
SOCIETY, 421 (1975). Here, several environmental organizations had
successfully sought an injunction directing the Department of the
Interior to perform legally required environmental analyses, and
properly to apply federal land use laws, in connection with oil companies'
application for permission to construct the Alaska Pipeline connecting
the newly discovered oil fields of Alaska's North Slope to the port of
Valdez. Because the plaintiffs had acted to vindicate "important rights of
all citizens" by bringing an action to ensure that the government system
functioned   properly,   the   DC   Circuit   found   them   entitled   to
reimbursement for "the reasonable value of their services." Alaska
Wilderness Soc. v. Morton, 495 F.2d 1026, 1032 (D.C. Cir.1974) (en banc).
Otherwise, the court reasoned, the cost of such litigation—especially
against well-financed parties such as Alyeska—might deter private
parties from seeking to have environmental statutes properly enforced.
Statutorily precluded from entering such an award against the United
States, the court held that the pipeline company Alyeska, an intervenor
supporting the government's (wrongful) approval of its pipeline, was
responsible for half of those costs.

Justice White, the dissenter in *Hall,* now wrote for a majority, emphasizing the need for legislative action given Congress' longstanding general endorsement of the American rule.

> In the United States, the prevailing litigant is ordinarily not entitled to collect a reasonable attorneys' fee from the loser. We are asked to fashion a far-reaching exception to this "American Rule"; but having considered its origin and development, we are convinced that it would be inappropriate for the Judiciary, without legislative guidance, to reallocate the burdens of litigation in the manner and to the extent urged by respondents and approved by the Court of Appeals. . . .

> We do not purport to assess the merits or demerits of the "American Rule" with respect to the allowance of attorneys' fees. It has been criticized in recent years, and courts have been urged to find exceptions to it. It is also apparent from our national experience that the encouragement of private action to implement public policy has been viewed as desirable in a variety of circumstances. But the rule followed in our courts with respect to attorneys' fees has survived. It is deeply rooted in our history and in congressional policy; and it is not for us to invade the legislature's province by redistributing litigation costs in the manner suggested by respondents and followed by the Court of Appeals.

421 U.S. at 247, 263–4, 270–1. Justices Marshall and Brennan dissented, relying on the "traditional equitable power" that had been recognized in *Hall.* Neither opinion mentioned the expenses for expert witnesses that (as in *Bradley*) had often been an element of "attorneys' fee" awards.

During the brief interval between decision in *Alyeska* and the passage of legislation directly responsive to that decision, and generally disapproving of it, Congress enacted the Education for All Handicapped Children Act of 1975. [EAHCA; The EAHCA is sometimes referred to as the Education of the Handicapped Act, EHA.] This lengthy and complex statute provided comprehensively for federal subvention of state expenses for the education of mentally and physically handicapped children, *on condition that* the states receiving this federal money accepted federal standards. The EAHCA standards included requirements that states establish administrative procedures to resolve any disputes about the services parents claimed for their children. Section 615(e)(2) of the Act, 20 U.S.C. § 1415(e)(2), authorized judicial review of local school boards' adverse administrative decisions, permitting the reviewing court to grant "appropriate" relief:

> In any action brought under this paragraph the court shall receive the records of the administrative proceedings, shall hear additional evidence at the request of a party, and, basing its decision on the preponderance of the evidence, shall grant such relief as the court determines is appropriate.

Within a few months of this statute Congress responded to Justice White's invitation by authorizing attorney's fee reimbursement for both environmental actions like the Wilderness Society's and, as relevant here, civil rights actions. The Civil Rights Attorney's Fees Awards Act of 1976, 42 U.S.C. § 1988 as amended, [CRAFA] provided in pertinent part:

> In any action or proceeding to enforce a provision of Sections 1977, 1978, 1979, 1980, and 1981 of the Revised Statutes [Sections 1981, 1982, 1983, 1985 and 1988 of U.S.C. Title 42] . . . the court, in its discretion, may allow the prevailing party, other than the United States, a reasonable attorney's fee as part of the costs.

Two years later, it provided for attorney's fee reimbursement under a more general statute dealing with the rights of mentally and physically handicapped persons to equal treatment, amending the Rehabilitation Act of 1973 by adding Section 505(b), 29 U.S.C. § 794a(b):

> In any action or proceeding to enforce or charge a violation of a provision of this subchapter, the court, in its discretion, may allow the prevailing party, other than the United States, a reasonable attorney's fee as part of the costs.

The "subchapter" in question, "Rights and Remedies," included Section 504, 29 U.S.C. § 794, "Non-discrimination under federal grants and programs," which begins

> (a) No otherwise qualified individual with a disability in the United States, as defined in section 705(20) of this title, shall, solely by reason of her or his disability, be excluded from the participation in, be denied the benefits of, or be subjected to discrimination under any program or activity receiving Federal financial assistance.

When parents who had successfully challenged a school board's rejection of their child's need for special education sought reimbursement of their attorney's fees, SMITH V. ROBINSON, RHODE ISLAND ASSOCIATE COMMISSIONER OF EDUCATION, 468 U.S. 992 (1984) reaffirmed *Alyeska* and denied relief. Despite the many intervening statutory changes in response to *Alyeska*, it emphasized the need for Congress to be explicit in effecting any departures from "the American Rule." Again (although one might know that expenses for psychologists would be central to any disputes over a child's special education needs) only "attorneys' fees" were discussed. Justice Brennan bitterly dissented for himself and Justices Marshall and Stevens:

> . . . [W]ith today's decision coming as it does after Congress has spoken on the subject of attorney's fees, Congress will now have to take the time to revisit the matter. And until it does, the handicapped children of this country whose difficulties are compounded by discrimination and by other deprivations of constitutional rights will have to pay the costs. It is at best ironic

that the Court has managed to impose this burden on handicapped children in the course of interpreting a statute wholly intended to promote the educational rights of those children.

At 1030–31.

PROBLEM

Two years later, Congress *did* revisit the matter, enacting the brief statute next presented. Does it authorize the reimbursement of the fees prevailing parents paid a consulting psychologist, in addition to their attorney's fee *simpliciter,* in a dispute over their child's placement? Her testing and testimony would be, if anything, more important than an attorney's help in successfully contesting the adequacy of a school board's provision for their child's special education needs. In considering the problem, start again just with the statutory text, to identify its possibilities of meaning. Be careful to consider the whole of the statute and the interrelation of its parts.

The Handicapped Children's Protection Act of 1986

SHORT TITLE

SEC. 1.   This Act may be cited as the "Handicapped Children's Protection Act of 1986".

AWARD OF ATTORNEYS' FEES

SEC. 2.   Section 615(e)(4) of the Education of the Handicapped Act is amended by inserting "(A)" after the paragraph designation and by adding at the end thereof the following new subparagraphs:

"(B) In any action or proceeding brought under this subsection, the court, in its discretion, may award reasonable attorneys' fees as part of the costs to the parents or guardian of a handicapped child or youth who is the prevailing party.

"(C) For the purpose of this subsection, fees awarded under this subsection shall be based on rates prevailing in the community in which the action or proceeding arose for the kind and quality of services furnished. No bonus or multiplier may be used in calculating the fees awarded under this subsection.

"(D) No award of attorneys' fees and related costs may be made in any action or proceeding under this subsection for services performed subsequent to the time of a written offer of settlement to a parent or guardian, if—

"i)   the offer is made within the time prescribed by Rule 68 of the Federal Rules of Civil Procedure or, in the case of an administrative proceeding, at any time more than ten days before the proceeding begins;

"ii)   the offer is not accepted within ten days; and

"iii) the court or administrative officer finds that the relief finally obtained by the parents or guardian is not more favorable to the parents or guardian than the offer of settlement.

"(E) Notwithstanding the provisions of subparagraph (D), an award of attorneys' fees and related costs may be made to a parent or guardian who is the prevailing party and who was substantially justified in rejecting the settlement offer.

"(F) Whenever the court finds that—

"i)   the parent or guardian, during the course of the action or proceeding, unreasonably protracted the final resolution of the controversy;

"ii) the amount of the attorneys' fees otherwise authorized to be awarded unreasonably exceeds the hourly rate prevailing in the community for similar services by attorneys of reasonably comparable skill, experience, and reputation; or "iii) the time spent and legal services furnished were excessive considering the nature of the action or proceeding

the court shall reduce, accordingly, the amount of the attorneys' fees awarded under this subsection.

"(G) The provisions of subparagraph (F) shall not apply in any action or proceeding if the court finds that the State or local educational agency unreasonably protracted the final resolution of the action or proceeding or there was a violation of section 615 of this Act.".

EFFECT OF EDUCATION OF THE HANDICAPPED ACT ON OTHER LAWS

SEC. 3.   Section 615 of the Education of the Handicapped Act is amended by adding at the end thereof the following new subsection.

"(f) Nothing in this title shall be construed to restrict or limit the rights, procedures, and remedies available under the Constitution, title V of the Rehabilitation Act of 1973, or other Federal statutes protecting the rights of handicapped children and youth, except that before the filing of a civil action under such laws seeking relief that is also available under this part, the procedures under subsections (b)(2) and (c) shall be exhausted to the same extent as would be required had the action been brought under this part."

GAO STUDY OF ATTORNEYS' FEES PROVISION

SEC. 4.   (a) The Comptroller General of the United States, through the General Accounting Office, shall conduct a study of the impact of the amendments to the Education of the Handicapped Act made under section 2 of this Act. Not later than June 30, 1989, the Comptroller General shall submit a report containing the findings of such study to the Committee on Education and Labor of the House of Representatives and the Committee on Labor and Human Resources of the Senate. The Comptroller General shall conduct a formal briefing for such Committees on the status of the study not later than March 1, 1988. Such report shall include the information described in subsection (b).

(b) The report authorized under subsection (a) shall include the following information:

(1) The number, in the aggregate and by State, of written decisions under section 615 (b)(2) and (c) transmitted to State advisory panels under section 615(d)(4) for fiscal years 1984 through 1988, the prevailing party in each such decision, and the type of complaint. For fiscal year 1986, the report shall designate which decisions concern complaints filed after the date of the enactment of this Act.

(2) the number, in the aggregate and by State, of civil actions brought under section 615(e)(2), the prevailing party in each action, and the type of complaint for fiscal years 1984 through 1988. For fiscal year 1986 the report shall designate which decisions concern complaints filed after the date of enactment.

(3) Data, for a geographically representative selective sample of states, indicating (A) the specific amount of attorneys' fees, costs, and expenses awarded to the prevailing party, in each action and proceeding under section 615(e)(4)(B) from the date of the enactment of this Act through fiscal year 1988, and the range of such fees, costs, and expenses awarded in the actions and proceedings under such section, categorized by type of complaint and (B) for the same sample as in (A) the number of hours spent by personnel, including attorneys and consultants, involved in the action or proceeding, and expenses incurred by the parents and the State educational agency and local educational agency.

(4) Data, for a geographically representative sample of States, on the experience of educational agencies in resolving complaints informally under section 615(b)(2), from the date of the enactment of this Act through fiscal year 1988.

EFFECTIVE DATE

SEC. 5. The amendment made by section 2 shall apply with respect to actions or proceedings brought under section 615(e) of the Education of the Handicapped Act after July 3, 1984, and actions or proceedings brought prior to July 4, 1984, under such section which was pending on July 4, 1984.

LEGISLATIVE HISTORY OF THE HANDICAPPED CHILDREN'S PROTECTION ACT OF 1986

The following legislative materials reflect the 1986 Act's progress through Congress, and are broadly representative of what an interested member of the public following the public proceedings could have learned about the statute.

Please be prepared to say

- Whether, and if so how, the *text* of the Handicapped Children's Act of 1986 could be understood to include permission to courts to order reimbursement of expert witness fees incurred by parents in successful actions to compel reluctant school boards to afford their children educational services to which they were entitled.

- What appear to have been the principal issues in controversy in Congress, and how they were resolved.

- Whether and in what respects these public records of what transpired may not fully reflect understandings held by important actors, such as committee chairs

- Can you find examples where the legislative history purports to resolve matters important to the debates, in a manner not readily supported by the enacted text?

- How, concretely, these materials reflect expectations about how they will be used, *after* the bill has been enacted, by people (citizens, lawyers, administrators, judges) attempting to ascribe meaning to the enacted text.

- To what if any extent the question of reimbursing prevailing parents for expert witness fees was addressed. What arguments do you find, or can you imagine, for or against such reimbursements? If you were planning testimony or lobbying activity for or against these bills, on behalf either of parent/student representatives or school board representatives, or if you were advising a Member about his forthcoming remarks in debate, would you have recommended any different course of action respecting this matter than you find? Why or why not?

I. HEARINGS

Committees in both House and Senate held hearings on legislation to overrule *Smith* within a year of the decision. The House hearings are not conveniently available. In the Senate, subcommittee chair Weicker (R. Conn.) and three other Senators appeared in support of the bill, and Senator Thurmond (R. S.C.) made a brief appearance counseling caution (but not opposition) in light of possible financial consequences. Two panels testified on behalf of proponents of the measure; the committee called no opponents as witnesses. The National Association of School Boards, however, was in the audience and submitted a statement suggesting concerns with both possible financial consequences for local boards required to fund parents' attorneys, and the impact of funding on the nature of the underlying process—that it might become more adversarial.

Senator Weicker's statement[2] reflects what you would find in the hearings overall—emphatic repudiation of *Smith,* attention to the importance and expense of attorneys, and no particular concern about the components of litigating cost. As close as one gets to detailed attention to the components of costs are statements like this one from the letter of The [Florida] Governor's Commission on Advocacy for Persons with Disabilities supporting the proposed draft:

> Unfortunately, legal process is also highly technical, costly, time consuming, and largely inaccessible to the average family. The extent of discovery and expert testimony that can be utilized in a typical educational due process hearing can rival a medical malpractice case."

Handicapped Children's Protection Act of 1985, Sen. Comm. on Labor and Human Resources, Subcomm. on the Handicapped 92, 93 (Thurs. May 16, 1985).

---

[2] "In their dissenting opinion to the *Smith v. Robinson* decision, Justices Brennan, Marshall and Stevens prophetically observe that, 'Congress will now have to take time to revisit the matter and until it does, the handicapped children of our country whose difficulties are compounded by discrimination and by other deprivations of constitutional rights, will have to pay the costs.'

"Today we are accepting that invitation to revisit the matter. It is clear to me that Justices Brennan, Marshall, and Stevens were correct; handicapped children are, indeed, paying the cost of the Court's misinterpretation of congressional intent. Unfortunately, they and their parents will continue to pay the cost until the Handicapped Children's Protection Act becomes law.

"In addition to being an incorrect interpretation of congressional intent, *Smith v. Robinson* is already having serious negative consequences for handicapped children. Enforcement of Public Law 94–142 depends largely on the individual initiative of parents who believe that their rights have been denied. Without any hope of recovering attorney's fees, even when they are absolutely right, most parents can no longer afford to pursue their rights in Federal Court.

"The bill that we are considering today is intended to be a simple restoration and clarification of congressional intent in enacting Public Law 94–142. In accomplishing that task S. 415 addresses three straightforward issues.

"First, Federal judges will have the discretion to award to prevailing parents reasonable attorney's fees associated with bringing their case to court.

"Second, nothing in Public Law 94–142 shall be construed to restrict or limit the rights, procedures, and remedies available to the parents of handicapped children under the Constitution, section 504, or other Federal statutes prohibiting discrimination.

"Third, the provisions of the amendment will be retroactive to include any actions or proceedings brought prior to, or pending at the time of the *Smith* v. *Robinson* decision."

II. S. 415

a. COMMITTEE REPORT

99TH CONGRESS	SENATE	REPORT
1st Session		99–112

Handicapped Children's Protection Act of 1985

JULY 25 (legislative day, July 16), 1985.—Ordered to be printed

MR. HATCH, from the Committee on Labor and Human Resources, submitted the following

REPORT

(To accompany S. 415) together with ADDITIONAL VIEWS

The Committee on Labor and Human Resources, to which was referred the bill (S. 415) to amend the Education of the Handicapped Act to authorize the award of reasonable attorneys' fees to certain prevailing parties; and to clarify the effect of the Education of the Handicapped Act on rights, procedures, and remedies under other laws relating to the prohibition of discrimination, having considered the same, reports favorably thereon with an amendment and recommends that the bill as amended do pass.

I. BACKGROUND OF S. 415

In passing the Education of All Handicapped Children Act of 1975 (Public Law 94–142) Congress indicated that "it is in the national interest that the Federal Government assist State and local efforts to provide programs to meet the educational needs of handicapped children in order to assure equal protection of the law." In those States which accept funds under Part B of the Education of the Handicapped Act [EHA], as amended by Public Law 94–142, the Act established an enforceable right to a free appropriate public education for all handicapped children and established due process procedures, including the right to judicial review, to protect those rights.

Congress' original intent was that due process procedures, including the right to litigation if that became necessary, be available to all parents. On July 5, 1984, the Supreme Court, in Smith v. Robinson, 468 U.S. 992, 104 S.Ct. 3457 (1984), determined that Congress intended that the EHA provide the exclusive source of rights and remedies in special education cases covered by that act. The effect of this decision was to preclude parents from bringing special education cases under section 504 of the Rehabilitation Act of 1973, and recovering attorney's fees available

under section 505 of that act, where relief was available under the
EHA. . . .

The situation which has resulted from the *Smith v. Robinson*
decision was summarized by Justices Brennan, Marshall, and Stevens in
their dissenting opinion: "Congress will now have to take the time to
revisit the matter." Seeking to clarify the intent of Congress with respect
to the educational rights of handicapped children guaranteed by the
EHA, the Handicapped Children's Protection Act of 1985 was introduced
on February 6, 1985. The Subcommittee on the Handicapped held a
hearing on March 16, 1985, to receive testimony from parents of
handicapped children, attorneys who have represented parents of
handicapped children in EHA litigation (including the *Smith v. Robinson*
case), and Edwin Martin, former Assistant Secretary of Education for
Special Education and Rehabilitative Services. Written testimony was
also received from the National School Boards Association and various
parent, advocacy, and professional education groups. On June 11, 1985,
the Subcommittee unanimously reported S. 415 with amendment to the
full Committee. On July 10, 1985, the full Committee unanimously
moved to order the bill, as amended, reported to the Senate.

II.   SECTION-BY-SECTION ANALYSIS

S. 415 as reported by the full Committee consists of six sections.
Throughout the remainder of this report the word "school" should be
interpreted to include State or local educational agencies or intermediate
educational units, as appropriate; the phrase "parent or legal
representative" includes a person acting as a parent of a child or a
surrogate parent who has been appointed in accordance with section
615(b)(1) of the EHA; and the words "reasonable attorney's fees" simply
mean fees appropriate in the circumstances of each case as determined
by court.

Section 1 provides that this Act be cited as the Handicapped
Children's Protection Act of 1985.

Section 2 provides for the award of reasonable attorney's fees to
prevailing parents in EHA civil actions and in administrative
proceedings to parents in certain specified circumstances.

Section 3 provides that the court cases will be heard de novo if
attorneys are not used at the due process hearing level.

Section 4 provides that the EHA does not limit the applicability of
other laws which protect handicapped children and youth except that
when a parent brings suit under another law when that suit could have
been brought under the EHA, the parent will be required to exhaust EHA
administrative remedies to the same degree as would have been required
had the suit been under the EHA.

Section 5 authorizes parent training centers under section 631 of the
EHA to train parents better to understand and participate in due process

proceedings and requires the establishment of at least one parent training center in each State.

Section 6 established a general effective date as the date of enactment and also authorizes courts retroactively to award attorney's fees for civil court actions to parents who prevailed in EHA cases pending on or brought after the date of the *Smith v. Robinson* decision.

IV. TABULATION OF VOTES CAST IN COMMITTEE

The motion to report the bill favorably to the Senate was passed unanimously by voice of the Committee. An earlier motion to strike the provision placing conditions upon fee awards for publicly funded attorneys who represent prevailing parents in EHA cases was defeated by a vote of 9 to 7.

V. REGULATORY IMPACT STATEMENT

The Committee has determined that there will be minimal increase in regulatory burden imposed by this bill. While new regulations will need to be promulgated to reflect the new provisions in the bill, those regulations build on existing regulations.

VI. CHANGES IN EXISTING LAW

In compliance with rule XXVI paragraph 12 of the Standard Rules of the Senate, the following provides a print of the statute or the part or section thereof to be amended or replaced (existing law proposed to be omitted is enclosed in black brackets, new matter is printed in italic, existing law in which no change is proposed is shown in roman):

EDUCATION OF THE HANDICAPPED ACT

* * *

PROCEDURAL SAFEGUARDS

SEC. 615. (a) Any State educational agency, any local educational agency, and any intermediate educational unit which receives assistance under this part shall establish and maintain procedures in accordance with subsection (b) through subsection (e) of this section to assure that handicapped children and their parents or guardians are guaranteed procedural safeguards with respect to the provision of free public education by such agencies and units.

(b) (1) The procedures required by this section shall include, but shall not be limited to—

(A) an opportunity for the parents or guardian of a handicapped child to examine all relevant records with respect to the identification, evaluation, and educational placement of the child and the provision of a free appropriate public education to such child and to obtain an independent education evaluation of the child;

(B) procedures to protect the rights of the child whenever the parents or guardian of the child are not known, unavailable, or the child is a ward of the State, including the assignment of an individual (who shall not be an employee of the State educational agency, local educational agency, or intermediate educational unit involved in the education or care of the child) to act as a surrogate for the parents or guardian;

(C) written prior notice to the parents or guardian of the child whenever such agency or unit—

(i)   proposes to initiate or change, or

(ii) refuses to initiate or change the identification, evaluation, or educational placement of the child or the provision of a free appropriate public education to the child;

(D) procedures designed to assure that the notice required by clause (C) fully inform the parents or guardian, in the parents' or guardian's native language, unless is not feasible to do so, of all procedures available pursuant to this section; and

(E) an opportunity to present complaints with respect to any matter relating to the identification, evaluation or educational placement of the child, or the provision of a free appropriate public education to such child.

(2) (A) Whenever a complaint has been received under paragraph (*l*) of this subsection, the parents or guardian shall have an opportunity for an impartial due process hearing which shall be conducted by the State educational agency or by the local educational agency or intermediate educational unit, as determined by State law or by the State educational agency. No hearing conducted pursuant to the requirements of this paragraph shall be conducted by an employee of such agency or unit involved in the education or care of the child.

(B) Within 5 days, after the receipt of a complaint under paragraph (1), the State or local educational agency or intermediate unit shall notify the parent or legal representative of the handicapped child or youth whether or not the State or local educational agency or intermediate educational unit, as the case may be, will use the services of an attorney in conjunction with the impartial due process hearing under this subsection, or the impartial review under subsection (c), in the manner described in section 615A(b)(1).

(c) If the hearing required in paragraph (2) of subsection (b) of this section is conducted by a local educational agency or an intermediate educational unit, any party aggrieved by the findings and decision rendered in such a hearing may appeal to the State education agency which shall conduct an impartial review of such hearing. The officer conducting such review shall make an independent decision upon completion of such review.

(d) Any party to any hearing conducted pursuant to subsections (b) and (c) shall be accorded (1) the right to be accompanied and advised by counsel and by individuals with special knowledge or training with respect to the problems of handicapped children, (2) the right to present evidence and confront, cross-examine, and compel the attendance of witnesses, (3) the right to a written or electronic verbatim record of such hearing, and (4) the right to written findings of fact and decisions (which findings and decisions shall also be transmitted to the advisory panel established pursuant to section 613(a)(12)).

(e) (1) A decision made in a hearing conducted pursuant to paragraph (2) of subsection (b) shall be final, except that any party involved in such hearing may appeal such decision under the provisions of subsection (c) and paragraph (2) of this subsection. A decision made under subsection (c) shall be final except that any party may bring an action under paragraph (2) of this subsection.

(2) (A) Any party aggrieved by the findings and decision made under subsection (b) who does not have the right to an appeal under subsection (c), and any party aggrieved by the findings and decision under subsection (c), shall have the rights to bring a civil action with respect to the complaint presented pursuant to this section, which action may be brought in any State court of competent jurisdiction or in a district court of the United States without regard to the amount in controversy. [In] *Except as provided in subparagraph (B), in* any action brought under this paragraph the court shall receive the records of the administrative proceedings, shall hear additional evidence at the request of a party and, basing its decision on the preponderance of the evidence, shall grant such relief as the court determines is appropriate.

(B) In any action brought under this paragraph in which no attorney participated in the hearing under subsection (b) or in review under subsection (c), the court shall hear the case de novo, but the trial de novo may not include the introduction of unrelated issues which the court determines would circumvent the exhaustion of administrative remedies.

(3) During the pendency of any proceedings conducted pursuant to this section, unless the State or local educational agency and the parents or guardian otherwise agree, the child shall remain in the then current educational placement of such child, or, if applying for initial admission to a public school, shall, with the consent of the parents or guardian be placed in the public school program until all such proceedings have been completed.

(4) The district courts of the United States shall have jurisdiction of actions brought under this subsection without regard to the amount of controversy.

(f)   The provisions of section 615A shall govern the award of a reasonable attorney's fee, reasonable witness fees, and other reasonable expenses in connection with any impartial due process hearing under subsection (b) of this section, any impartial review under subsection (c), and the bringing of the civil action under subsection (e).

(g)   Nothing in this title shall be construed to restrict or limit the rights, procedures, and remedies available under the Constitution, title V of the Rehabilitation Act of 1973, or other Federal statutes protecting the rights of handicapped children and youth, except that before the filing of a civil action under such laws seeking relief that is also available under this part, the procedures under subsection (b)(2) and (c) shall be exhausted to the same extent as would be required had the action been brought under this part.

FEES AND EXPENSES

Sec. 615A. (a)(1)(A) Except as provided in subparagraphs (B) and (C), in any civil action brought under section 615(e), the court may, in its discretion, award a reasonable attorney's fee, reasonable witness fees, and other reasonable expenses of the civil action, in addition to the costs to a parent or legal representative of a handicapped child or youth who is the prevailing party.

(B)   Whenever—

(i)   the decision of the impartial due process hearing under section 615(b) or the impartial review of such hearing under section 615(c) is in favor of the parent or legal representative of a handicapped child or youth, and

(ii) the State or local educational agency or intermediate educational unit appeals the decision pursuant to section 615(e), the parent or legal representative of the handicapped child or youth shall be awarded a reasonable attorney's fee, reasonable witness fees, and other reasonable expenses of the civil action.

(C)   Whenever—

(i)   the decision of the impartial due process hearing under section 615(b) or the impartial review of such hearing under section 615(c), and the decision of the courts, is in favor of the parent or legal representative of a handicapped child or youth, and

(ii) the State of local educational agency or intermediate educational unit appeals the decision of the courts pursuant to section 615(e)

the parent or legal representative of the handicapped child or youth shall be awarded a reasonable attorney's fees, reasonable witness fees, and other reasonable expenses of such appeal.

(2)   Whenever the parent or legal representative—

(A)   is awarded fees under subparagraph (A), (B), or (C), and

(B)   is represented by a publicly funded organization which provides legal services,

the reasonable attorney's fee which is awarded pursuant to this subsection shall be computed based upon the actual cost related to the bringing of the civil action under section 615(e) to the publicly funded organization, including the proportion of the compensation of the attorney so related, other reasonable expenses which can be documented, and the proportion of the annual overhead costs of the publicly funded organization attributable to the number of hours reasonably spent on such civil action.

(b)   (1)   If the State or local educational agency, or intermediate educational unit, determines, after the receipt of a complaint under section 615(b)(1), to use the services of an attorney in conjunction with the impartial due process hearing under section 615(b)(2), or the impartial review under section 615(c), for consultation, preparation, presentation of written or oral argument, or evidence, then the State or local educational agency or intermediate educational unit, as the case may be shall—

(A)   notify the parent or legal representative of the handicapped child or youth of its intention to use an attorney in the manner described in this subsection as required by section 615(b)(2)(B);

(B)   furnish to the parent or legal representative of such a child or youth a list of attorneys who practice in the area in which the handicapped child or youth resides, and who are knowledgeable about special education law, regulations, and procedures; and

(C)   pay the costs of the State or local education agency or intermediate educational unit, as the case may be, and the costs of the parent or legal representative of the handicapped child or youth, for reasonable attorneys' fees, reasonable witness fees, and other reasonable expenses related to the hearing or review, as the case may be.

(2)   If the parent or legal representative of the handicapped child or youth determines—

(A)   after filing a complaint under section 615(b)(2) and after receiving notification from the State or local educational agency or intermediate educational unit under section 615(b)(2) that the State or local educational agency or intermediate educational unit will not use an attorney; or

(B)   after the filing of a complaint under section 615(b)(2) and prior to the notification of the State or local educational

agency or intermediate educational unit under section 615(b)(2)(B),

to use the services of an attorney in conjunction with the impartial due process hearing under section 615(b)(2), or the impartial review under section 615(b)(c), for consultation, preparation, presentation of written or oral argument or evidence, then—

> (i) the parent or legal representative shall notify the State, local educational agency, or intermediate educational unit, as the case may be within 5 days after receipt of the notification of such agency or unit under section 615(b)(2)(B) of their intention to use an attorney in the manner described in this subsection;

> (ii) the parent or legal representative of the handicapped child or youth shall pay the cost of attorneys' fees, witness fees, and other expenses relating to the hearing or review, as the case may be, incurred by such parent or legal representative; and

> (iii) the State or local educational agency or intermediate educational unit shall pay the cost of attorneys' fees, witness fees, and other expenses incurred by the State or local educational agency or intermediate educational unit, as the case may be.

(3) If the State or local educational agency or intermediate educational unit determines not to use the services of an attorney in conjunction with the due process hearing under section 615(b)(2), or the impartial hearing review under section 615(c), in the manner described in paragraph (1), the State or local educational agency or intermediate educational unit, as the case may be, shall—

> (A) notify the parent or legal representative of the handicapped child or youth as required by section 615(b)(2)(B); and—

> (B) furnish to the parent or legal representative of such a child or youth a list of parent training centers, Protection and Advocacy Agencies, and other organizations, which are located in the area in which the handicapped child or youth resides, and which are knowledgeable about special education law, regulations, and procedures.

* * *

VII. ADDITIONAL VIEWS OF SENATORS HATCH, WEICKER, STAFFORD, DOLE, PELL, MATSUNAGA, SIMON, KERRY, KENNEDY, METZENBAUM, DODD, AND GRASSLEY

While the full committee (at the markup of July 10, 1985) voted unanimously to report S. 415 as amended, there were numerous expressions of concerns that further work would need to be done prior to Senate consideration of the bill.

As a result, Senator Hatch, as chairman of the full committee and Senator Weicker, as chairman of the Subcommittee on the Handicapped, met with representatives of the administration and other interested parties, and, with the agreement of the Department of Education decided to offer an amendment in the form of a substitute when S. 415 is considered on the Senate floor. This amended version of S. 415 is considered by Senators Stafford, Dole, Pell, Matsunaga, Simon, Kerry, Kennedy, Metzenbaum, Dodd, and Grassley.

Throughout remainder of this section of the report the word "school" should be interpreted to include State or local educational agencies or intermediate educational units, as appropriate; the phrase "parent or legal representative" includes a person acting as a parent of a child or a surrogate parent who has been appointed in accordance with section 615(b)(1)(B) of the EHA; and the words "reasonable attorney's fees" simply mean fees appropriate in the circumstances of each case as determined by the Court.

SECTION-BY-SECTION ANALYSIS OF PROPOSED AMENDMENT

The bill described below, which will be offered as an amendment in the nature of a substitute to S. 415 on the Senate floor, is similar to the original version of S. 415, introduced on February 6, 1985, with two substantive additions. A section-by-section analysis of the substitute amendment to be offered on the Senate floor follows.

Section 1 provides that this Act may be known as the Handicapped Children's Protection Act of 1985.

Section 2 provides the award of reasonable attorney fees to prevailing parents in an EHA action or proceeding. In those cases where the prevailing parent is represented by an attorney who is employed by an organization which receives its operating expenses from Federal, State, or local governmental sources for the purpose of providing legal services, the organization shall be compensated based on the organization's costs.

Section 3 provides that the EHA does not limit the applicability of other laws which protect handicapped children and youth, except that when a parent brings suit under another law when that suit could have been brought under the EHA, the parent will be required to exhaust EHA administrative remedies to the same degree as would have been required had the suit been brought under the EHA.

Section 4 authorizes courts to award attorney's fees in conjunction with any EHA action or proceeding brought after July 3, 1984, or brought before July 4, 1984, but still pending on July 4, 1984. This provision would thus apply to cases brought on or pending on the date of the *Smith v. Robinson* decision.

DISCUSSION OF SUBSTITUTE BILL

GENERAL

The Committee believes that the substitute bill provides fee awards to handicapped children on a basis similar to other fee shifting statutes when securing the right guaranteed to them by the EHA.

AWARD OF FEES AND EXPENSES

Section 2 of the bill amends section 615(e)(4) of the EHA to permit a court, in its discretion, to award reasonable attorney's fees to parents or legal representatives of a handicapped child or youth who is the prevailing party in any action or proceeding brought under this subsection.

It is the committee's intention that a parent or legal representative should be free to select and be represented by the attorney of his/her choice.

The committee understands and intends that State and local agencies may not use funds made available to them under part B of the EHA to pay attorney's fees or other costs incurred by parents that a court assesses against those agencies under the bill. Using these funds for those costs would divert scarce resources from direct services to handicapped children.

It is the committee's intent that the terms "prevailing party" and "reasonable" be construed consistent with the U.S. Supreme Court's decision in Hensley v. Eckerhart, 461 U.S. 424, 440 (1983). In this case, the Court held that:

> the extent of a plaintiff's success is a crucial factor in determining the proper amount of an award of attorney's fees. Where the plaintiff has failed to prevail on a claim that is distinct in all respects from his successful claims, the hours spent on the unsuccessful claim should be excluded in considering the amount of a reasonable fee. Where a lawsuit consists of related claims, a plaintiff who has won substantial relief should not have his attorney's fee reduced simply because the district court did not adopt each contention raised. But where the plaintiff achieved only limited success, the district court should award only that amount of fees that is reasonable in relation to the results obtained.

It is also the committee's intent that, consistent with section 300.10 of Title 34 (EHA regulations) the term "parent or legal representative" includes a person acting as a parent of a child or a surrogate parent who has been appointed in accordance with section 615(b)(1)(B) of the EHA. The term does not include the State if the child is a ward of the State. Under appropriate circumstances, a child or youth may also bring an action under the EHA and receive an award of attorney's fees to the extent that he/she prevails.

The committee also intends that section 2 should be interpreted consistent with fee provisions of statutes such as title VII of Civil Rights Act of 1964 which authorizes courts to award fees for time spent by counsel in mandatory administrative proceedings under those statutes. See New York Gaslight Club, Inc. v. Carey, 447 U.S. 54 (1980), (compare Webb v. Board of Education for Dyer County, 471 U.S. 234 (1985) in which the court declined to award fees for work done at the administrative level because the statute under which the suit was brought did not require the exhaustion of administrative remedies prior to going to court).

The committee intends that S. 415 will allow the Court, but not the hearing officer, to award fees for time spent by counsel in mandatory EHA administrative proceedings. This is consistent with the committee's position that handicapped children should be provided fee awards on a basis similar to other fee shifting statutes when securing the rights guaranteed to them by the EHA.

It is the intention of the committee to adopt the policy of Christiansburg Garment Co. v. EEOC, 434 U.S. 412 (1978), which is that a party which brings an action that is "frivolous, unreasonable, or without foundation" may be held liable for the prevailing defendant's attorney fees. Nothing in S. 415 should override this established principle concerning frivolous lawsuits. While the committee has no evidence that parents bring EHA suits which are frivolous, unreasonable, or without foundation, in the rare instance where this occurs, this provision would apply.

The committee included subsection (c) to ensure that in those cases where the prevailing party is represented by an attorney who is employed by an organization which receives funds, other than attorney fees awards, from Federal, State, or local governmental sources, the party should be awarded fees on the basis of the actual costs of the litigation to the organization. This limits "double-dipping" or providing attorney fee awards out of governmental funds to organizations already receiving some funding from governmental sources.

EFFECTIVE DATE OF ENACTMENT

The bill would be effective on enactment. However, the bill also provides that parents who filed after Smith v. Robinson or whose action or proceeding was pending at the time of Smith v. Robinson may be awarded fees on the same grounds as parents whose action or proceeding is brought after the enactment of S. 415.

TEXT OF AMENDMENT PROPOSED TO BE SUBSTITUTED FOR COMMITTEE REPORTED VERSION OF S. 415

S. 415

To amend the Education of the Handicapped Act to authorize the award of reasonable attorneys' fees to certain prevailing parties, and to clarify the effect of the Education of the Handicapped Act on rights, procedures, and remedies under other laws relating to the prohibition of discrimination.

In lieu of the matter proposed to be inserted by the committee amendment insert the following:

That this Act may be cited as the "Handicapped Children's Protection Act of 1985".

Sec. 2. Section 615(e)(4) of the Education of the Handicapped Act amended by inserting "(A)" after the paragraph designation and by adding at the end thereof the following new subparagraphs:

"(B) In any action or proceeding brought under this subsection, the court, in its discretion, may award a reasonable attorney's fee in addition to the costs to a parent or legal representative of a handicapped child or youth who is the prevailing party.

"(C) Whenever the parent or legal representative of a handicapped child or youth—

(i) is awarded fees under subparagraph (B), and

(ii) is represented by a publicly funded organization which provides legal services,

the reasonable attorney's fee which is awarded pursuant to this subsection shall be computed based upon the actual cost related to the bringing of the civil action under this subsection to the publicly funded organization, including the proportion of the compensation of the attorney so related, other reasonable expenses which can be documented, and the proportion of the annual overhead costs of the publicly funded organization attributable to the number of hours reasonably spent on such civil action.

"(D) For the purpose of this paragraph, the term 'publicly funded organization' means any organization which receives funds, other than attorney fee awards, from Federal, State, or local governmental sources which are available for use during any fiscal year in which the action or proceeding is pending to enable the organization to provide legal counsel or representation."

Sec. 3. Section 615 of the Education of the Handicapped Act is amended by adding at the end thereof the following new subsection:

"(f) Nothing in this title shall be construed to restrict or limit the rights, procedures, and remedies available under the Constitution, title V of the Rehabilitation Act of 1973, or other Federal statutes protecting the rights of handicapped children and youth, except that before the filing of a civil action under such laws seeking relief that is also available under this part, the procedures under subsections (b)(2) and (c) shall be exhausted to the same extent as would be required had the action been brought under this part."

Sec. 4.   The amendment made by section 2 shall apply with respect to actions or proceedings brought under section 615(e) of the Education of the Handicapped Act after July 3, 1984, and actions or proceedings brought prior to July 4, 1984, under such section which were pending on July 4, 1984.

VIII. ADDITIONAL VIEWS OF KERRY, KENNEDY, PELL, DODD, SIMON, METZENBAUM, AND MATSUNAGA

Although strongly endorsing the principle that parents or legal representatives of handicapped children must be able to access the full range of available remedies in order to protect their handicapped children's educational rights, seven members of the committee (Kerry, Kennedy, Pell, Dodd, Simon, Metzenbaum, and Matsunaga) believe that one provision should be deleted from the legislation. Language exists in the bill which limits attorney's fees available to nonprofit, publicly funded organizations who provide legal assistance, yet will not limit fees to privately funded attorneys. Undoubtedly, this creates a blatant double standard which will have a particularly negative impact on lower income handicapped children most dependent on legal representation by publicly funded attorneys. Furthermore, by requiring that attorneys' fees awarded to publicly funded attorneys be computed according the cost based standard rather than the prevailing market based standard used by private attorneys, a dangerous precedent for all future cases litigated in this area will be set.

b.   SENATE DEBATES

131 Congressional Record (Senate)
Tuesday, July 30, 1985; (Legislative day of Tuesday, July 16, 1985)
99th Cong. 1st Sess. 131 Cong. Rec. S. 10396, 10465

EDUCATION OF THE HANDICAPPED ACT AMENDMENTS; WEICKER (AND OTHERS) AMENDMENT NO. 561

Mr. DOLE (for Mr. Weicker, for himself, Mr. Hatch, Mr. Kennedy, Mr. Dole, Mr. Stafford, Mr. Grassley, Mr. Pell, Mr. Simon, Mr. Metzenbaum, and Mr. Dodd) proposed an amendment to the bill (S. 415) to amend the Education of the Handicapped Act to authorize the award of reasonable attorneys' fees to certain prevailing parties, and to clarify the effect of the Education of the Handicapped Act on rights, procedures, and remedies under other laws relating to prohibition of discrimination; as follows:

[The text of the substitute set out in VII of the Committee Report was printed here, with a slight change unimportant to our consideration.]

Mr. WEICKER. Mr. President, I rise today to offer an amendment in the form of a substitute bill to S. 415 as it was reported out of the Labor and Human Resources Committee on July 10, 1985. This amendment is cosponsored by Senators Hatch, Stafford, Grassley, Dole, Kennedy,

Kerry, Pell, Metzenbaum, Dodd, Matsunaga, and Simon, and has been developed in conjunction with and agreed to by the Department of Education and the Department of Justice. The passage of this substitute bill will bring to fruition months of intensive work and negotiation among Senators and Representatives of the administration. The bill reverses the Supreme Court's Smith versus Robinson decision of July 5, 1984. In that decision, the Court ruled, contrary to the original intent of Congress, that Public Law 94–142 does not allow the award of attorney's fees to parents who, after exhausting administrative procedures, prevail in a civil court action to protect their child's right to a free appropriate public education. The Court's decision also raised questions about the extent to which rights, remedies, and procedures available under section 504 of the Rehabilitation Act and other Federal civil rights statutes will be applicable to claims made under the Education of the Handicapped Act [EHA].

The purpose of S. 415 is simple—to overturn the Smith versus Robinson decision and thereby to clarify congressional intent regarding these matters. The fact that Congress did not intend to leave unprotected the rights of handicapped children and their parents to secure the free appropriate public education promised to them by EHA was made clear in the 1978 passage of section 505(b) of the Rehabilitation Act which makes attorney's fees available under section 504. Section 505(b) clearly does not make an exception for handicapped children seeking an appropriate education. Indeed, the 1978 Senate and House reports accompanying section 505(b) explain that disabled individuals were one of the very few minority groups in this country who had not been specifically authorized by Congress to seek attorney's fees. The purpose of section 505(b) was "to correct this omission and thereby assist handicapped individuals in securing the legal protection guaranteed them."

Unfortunately, because the Court, in Smith versus Robinson, misinterpreted Congress' intent, handicapped children are now provided substantially less protection against discrimination than other vulnerable groups of people. S. 415 would remove these inequities by restoring equivalent protection to handicapped children, a group undeniably deserving congressional protection.

Allowing courts to award attorney's fees to prevailing plaintiffs is not an unusual congressional remedy. In fact, according to the Congressional Research Service (Rept. No. 85–126A), Congress has already enacted more than 130 fee shifting statutes which provide for the award of attorneys' fees to parties who prevail in court to obtain what is guaranteed to them by law. Many of these statutes are civil rights statutes—that is, Age Discrimination Employment Act through 29 U.S.C. sec. 626(b); the Equal Pay Act through 29 U.S.C. sec. 216(b); the Fair Housing Act through 42 U.S.C. sec. 3612(c); title II and title VII of the Civil Rights Act of 1964 through 42 U.S.C. sec. 2000a–3(b) and

2000e–5(k); and the Civil Rights Attorney's Fees Awards Act of 1976 through 42 U.S.C. sec. 1988; but similar attorney's fees statutes exist for a wide variety of laws ranging from the Safe Drinking Water Act through 42 U.S.C. sec. 300j–8(d), to the Deepwater Ports Act through 33 U.S.C. sec. 1515(d), to the National Historic Preservation Act through 16 U.S.C. sec. 470w–4.

With this amendment, S. 415 will enable courts to compensate parents for whatever reasonable cost they had to incur to fully secure what was guaranteed to them by the EHA. As in other fee shifting statutes, it is our intent that such awards will include, at the discretion of the court, reasonable attorney's fees, necessary expert witness fees, and other reasonable expenses which were necessary for parent to vindicate their claim to a free appropriate public education for their handicapped child.

The compromise bill which was unanimously agreed to by the full committee contained a provision which limits the amount of the award made to prevailing parents who are represented by a publicly funded organization. The amendment being offered today contains the same provision, but clarifies that the words "publicly funded organization" only refer to those organizations, such as a Legal Services, Inc., which receive Federal, State, or local governments funds which are specifically available to provide legal counsel or representation to parents of handicapped children in EHA-related cases. It does not include organizations which only receive Government funds for other specific purposes, when that money is not available for representing parents of handicapped children in EHA cases.

Mr. President, I urge my colleagues to support this important piece of legislation which will restore to parents of handicapped children the right to be awarded attorney fees and other reasonable expenses when they must go to court to secure the educational rights promised to them by Congress. By restoring this right we will once again demonstrate that handicapped people should be accorded the same protections as all other citizens of our Nation.

Mr. STAFFORD. Mr. President, I rise in support of S. 415, the Handicapped Children's Protection Act of 1985.

Critics of S. 415 are fearful that the availability of attorney's fees awards to prevailing parents will increase litigation. It is my belief that the opposite situation will occur. State and local education agencies will be more inclined to work out effective compromises with parents before court action becomes necessary.

Parents must have every opportunity to participate with local school personnel to develop programs for their handicapped children if 94–142 is to provide the free and appropriate education that it promised. That includes making reasonable legal fees available if the services of an attorney are necessary.

A law that mandates a free and appropriate public education to handicapped children, that at the same time denies the awarding of legal fees incurred to uphold that mandate, is a hollow promise at best. It hurts the families most that can least afford it.

I urge my colleagues to vote in favor of S. 415. Senator Weicker is to be commended for his leadership on this important legislation.

Mr. HATCH. Mr. President, S. 415, the Handicapped Children's Protection Act, was drafted in response to the Supreme Court's 1984 opinion in Smith versus Robinson.

The Hatch-Weicker substitute we are considering today is a modification of the committee bill reported by my Labor and Human Resources Committee on July 10. It is similar to S. 415 as originally introduced with two substantive changes. The first requires exhaustion of administration remedies before pursuing litigation. The second places conditions upon fee awards for publicly funded attorneys representing parents who prevailed in EHA cases.

Mr. KENNEDY. Mr. President, I rise in strong support of this important bill that is before us today.

Mr. KERRY. Mr. President, I would like to rise in strong support of S. 415 the Handicapped Children's Protection Act and urge that my colleagues join me in passing this vital legislation. The bill is designed to ensure that all parents or legal guardians of handicapped children are able to fully access the available remedies to protect their handicapped children's educational rights.

As a cosponsor of S. 415, 1 strongly endorse the principles of rights to education for all handicapped children. However, there is one provision in the legislation which greatly undermines the strength of this bill and should be deleted. Language exists in the bill which limits attorneys' fees available to nonprofit, publicly funded organizations who provide legal services, yet will not place these same limitations on privately funded attorneys. To some this is considered double dipping; quite frankly Mr. President I view this as a double standard. This blatant double standard will have a particularly negative impact on lower income handicapped children most dependent on legal representation by publicly funded attorneys. Furthermore, requiring that attorneys' fees awarded to publicly funded attorneys be computed according to a cost-based standard rather than the prevailing market-based standard used by private attorneys, will set a dangerous precedent for all future cases litigated in this area.

In addition, I would like to point out that families most in need of reimbursement of attorneys fees are families most likely to turn to public advocacy for assistance. Furthermore, money awarded to publicly funded attorneys is recycled back into the organization for which the attorney works to expand services to low-income individuals. As a lawyer who has worked in a public attorney's office, I have witnessed firsthand that under our present system, offices which provide legal assistance to indigent handicapped children encounter an overwhelming demand for their services and unfortunately have very limited resources to meet this demand. I emphatically believe that any additional funds made available to expand legal services to our Nation's disabled poor citizens is money well spent.

Mr. President, I offered an amendment in the Labor and Human Resources Committee that would have deleted the provision to cap publicly funded attorneys' fees. The amendment was narrowly defeated by a 7 to 9 vote. The closeness of this vote leads me to believe that this issue is not a decisive one, and that great need still exists to further examine the issue. S. 415 is designed to reinforce the rights to education for all handicapped children provided in Public Law 94–142 the Education of the Handicapped Act, including their rights to access the courts when education is being denied to them. In essence, by limiting the attorneys' fees to those who represent handicapped children who are poor, we are ultimately limiting the rights to an appropriate education for less fortunate handicapped children in this country. This double standard weakens the legislation and while I urge my colleagues to vote for the Handicapped Children's Protection Act, I strongly urge that when this bill goes to conference committee, that we do all we can to uphold the educational rights of all handicapped children, rich and poor, and delete this provision.

Mr. SIMON. Mr. President, 10 years ago, as a member of the House Education and Labor Committee, I was proud to be a cosponsor of the bill that became Public Law 94–142, the Education of All Handicapped Children Act. That act was intended to provide the program, procedures and rights that would end discrimination against handicapped children in public education. Today, I am pleased to be a cosponsor of S. 415, the Handicapped Children's Protection Act of 1985, which will give parents the ability to accomplish the goals of Public Law 94–142 for their children.

The Supreme Court's decision on July 5, 1984, in Smith versus Robinson, jeopardizes the educational rights provided under Public Law 94–142 and negates the intent of Congress to assure equal protection for all handicapped children. In eliminating a parent's ability to be reimbursed for attorney fees under Public Law 94–142, the Court has made the due process guarantees of that act, including the right to go to court when necessary, meaningless for all but the wealthy and well informed. By limiting the remedies available to parents under other statutes, the Court misinterpreted congressional intent to enhance, not replace, the rights of handicapped children under other laws.

The provisions of S. 415 reaffirm and clarify the original intent of Congress in providing a variety of effective avenues for parents to use in resolving questions concerning the appropriate educational services their handicapped children should receive. I would like to discuss two major aspects of this bill: the inclusion of the right to reimbursement for fees incurred during the administrative process; and the requirement that administrative proceedings be exhausted prior to court action.

The language of S. 415, which permits the award of a reasonable attorney fee in any action or proceeding brought under this subpart, is identical to the language of title VII of the Civil Rights Act of 1964, interpreted by the Supreme Court in NEW YORK GASLIGHT CLUB V. CAREY (447 U.S. 54) (1980). The Court stated:

> Congress' use of the broadly inclusive disjunctive phrase "action or proceeding" indicates an intent to subject the losing party to an award of attorney's fees and costs that includes expenses incurred for administrative proceedings.

Mr. President, I wish that I could endorse S. 415 without qualification. There is one provision, however, that does not deserve our support and which I am hopeful will be removed in conference with the House. Under this provision, any organization which receives public funds for the purpose of providing legal assistance would be eligible for attorney fee awards only in the amount that could be documented to be the actual cost of the case. Attorneys awarded fees under the many other fee-shifting statutes—including such wide-ranging statutes as the Deepwater Ports Act, the National Historic Preservation Act, the Equal Pay Act and the Fair Housing Act—may be compensated on the basis of the prevailing market-based standard used by private attorneys. A serious question must be raised as to why this limit is being imposed on handicapped cases and on the seriously inadequate legal services available to the poor. This provision will hurt most those whom this bill as a whole is most intended to help.

To put the inequity of this dual standard into perspective, I have calculated the cumulative loss of Federal funding for the Legal Services Corporation over the past 4 years as a result of its cut in fiscal year 1981. Based on CBO estimates of current service increases in those years, the total lost by the Legal Services Corporation has been $382 million. In contrast, if every penny of attorney fees awarded under this statute went to Legal Services—which would not happen—with an average award of $5,000, and 1,400 cases—far more than likely, but the total of both administrative and court hearings in 1983, the reimbursement would be less than 2 percent of the funds Legal Services has lost in the past 4 years.

Fees awarded to publicly funded organizations do not enrich the attorneys who work for those organizations. Instead, these funds increase the organizations' ability to help persons who too often have turned to them in desperation. Let us remember that the adoption of this provision will specifically reduce services for low-income parents seeking legal assistance to assure the rights of their handicapped children to an appropriate education.

I support prompt passage of this much needed legislation.

The PRESIDING OFFICER. The bill is open to further amendment. If there be no further amendment to be proposed, the question is on agreeing to the committee amendment in the nature of a substitute, as amended.

The committee amendment, as amended, was agreed to.

The bill was ordered to be engrossed for a third reading and was read the third time.

The PRESIDING OFFICER. The bill having been read the third time, the question is, Shall it pass?

So the bill (S. 415) was passed.

III. H.R. 1523

a.   REPORT

99TH CONGRESS	HOUSE OF	REPORT
1st Session	REPRESENTATIVES	99–296

Handicapped Children's Protection Act of 1985

October 2, 1985.—Committed to the Committee of the
Whole House on the State of the Union and ordered to
be printed

Mr. HAWKINS, from the Committee on Education and Labor,
submitted the following together with SUPPLEMENTAL VIEWS [To
accompany H.R. 1523]

[Including cost estimate of the Congressional Budget Office]

The Committee on Education and Labor, to whom was referred the
bill (H.R. 1523) to amend the Education of the Handicapped Act to
authorize the award of reasonable attorneys' fees to certain prevailing
parties, to clarify the effect of the Education of the Handicapped Act on
rights, procedures, and remedies under other laws relating to the
prohibition of discrimination, and for other purposes, having considered
the same, report favorably thereon with amendment and recommend
that the bill as amended do pass.

The amendment is as follows:

Strike out all after the enacting clause and insert in lieu thereof the
following:

SECTION 1. SHORT TITLE

This Act may be cited as the "Handicapped Children's Protection Act
of 1985".

SEC. 2.   AWARD OF ATTORNEYS' FEES.

Section 615(e)(4) of the Education of the Handicapped Act
(hereinafter in this Act referred to as the "Act") as amended by insetting
"(A)" after the paragraph designation and by adding at the end thereof
the following:

"(B) In any action or proceeding brought under this subsection, the
court, in its discretion, may award reasonable attorneys' fees, expenses,
and costs to the parents or guardian of a handicapped child or youth who
is the prevailing party.

(5) For purposes of this subsection—

"(A) fees awarded under this subsection shall be based on rates
prevailing in the community in which the action or proceeding arose
for the kind and quality of services furnished; and

"(B) fees, expenses, and costs awarded under this subsection to a prevailing part may not be paid with funds provided to the State under this Act.".

SEC. 3. EFFECT OF EDUCATION OF THE HANDICAPPED ACT ON OTHER LAWS.

(a) EFFECT ON OTHER LAWS.—Section 615 of the Act is amended by inserting at the end thereof the following new subsection:

"(f) Nothing in this title shall be construed to restrict or limit the rights, procedures, and remedies available under title V of the Rehabilitation Act of 1973 or other Federal laws redressing the rights of handicapped children and youth, except that before the filing of a civil action under such laws seeking relief that is also available under this part, the procedures under subsections (b)(2) and (c) shall be exhausted to the same extent as would be required had the action been brought under this part.".

(b) REGULATIONS UNDER SECTION 504 OF THE REHABILITATION ACT OF 1973.—With respect to preschool, elementary, secondary, and adult education programs and activities, section 504 of the Rehabilitation Act of 1973 shall be carried out in accordance with regulations under such section in effect on July 4, 1984; unless expressly authorized by Act or Joint Resolution of the Congress approved after July 4, 1984.

SEC. 4. IMPROVEMENTS IN PROCEDURAL SAFEGUARDS UNDER THE ACT.

(a) PUBLIC ACCESS TO HEARING DECISIONS.—Section 615(d)(4) of the Act is amended by inserting "shall be made available to the public consistent with the requirements of section 617(c) and" immediately before "shall also".

(b) INFORMAL COMPLAINT RESOLUTION PROCEDURE.—Section 615(b)(2) is amended—

(1) by striking out the first sentence and inserting in lieu thereof the following:

"Whenever a complaint has been received under paragraph (1) of this subsection, the parents or guardian shall be provided an opportunity to meet informally with the State or local educational agency or intermediate educational unit to resolve the complaint. If the complaint is not resolved satisfactorily or a decision is made not to meet informally, the parents or guardian shall have an opportunity for an impartial due process hearing which shall be conducted by the State educational agency, the local educational agency, or an intermediate educational unit as determined by State law or by the State educational agency."; and

(2) by inserting at the end of such paragraph the following new sentence:

"Any decision regarding participation in an informal meeting under this paragraph shall not affect the availability or provision of any rights of the parents or guardian under this section.".

(c) ANTI-RETALIATION PROVISION.—Section 615 of the Act is amended by inserting at the end thereof the following new subsection:

"(g) No person may discharge, intimidate, retaliate, threaten, coerce or otherwise take an adverse action against any person because such person has filed a complaint, testified, furnished information, assisted, or participated in any manner in a meeting, hearing, review, investigation, or other activity related to the administration of, exercise of authority under, or right secured by this part.".

SEC. 5. EFFECTIVE DATE.

(a) GENERAL PROVISION.—Except as provided in subsection (b), the provisions of this Act shall take effect on the date of enactment of this Act.

(b) LIMITED RETROACTIVE APPLICATION.—The amendments made by sections 2 and 3 shall apply with respect to actions or proceedings brought under section 615(e) of the Education of the Handicapped Act after July 3, 1984, and actions or proceedings brought prior to July 4, 1984, under such section which were pending on July 4, 1984.

COMMITTEE ACTION

On March 7, 1985 Congressman Williams introduced H.R. 1523, the Handicapped Children's Protection Act of 1985. On March 12 1985, the Subcommittee on Select Education held a hearing at which members of the Subcommittee heard testimony from the American Association of School Administrators, the National School Boards Association, the Council for Exceptional Children, the Consortium for Citizens with Developmental Disabilities, and a parent. On April 3, 1985, the Subcommittee marked-up the bill. On September 11th and 19th, 1985, the Committee on Education and Labor considered the bill and on the latter date ordered reported by voice vote an Amendment in the Nature of a Substitute.

BACKGROUND AND NEED FOR LEGISLATION

In 1971 and 1972 two landmark cases established the constitutional rights of handicapped children to a free appropriate public education. The courts found, among other things, that handicapped children's rights under 42 U.S.C. 1983 had been abridged. Section 1983 prohibits, among other things, an agency acting under color of state law from abridging a handicapped person's rights under the Constitution. The cases were and 343 F.Supp. 279 (E.D. Pa. 1972) and Mills v. Board of Education, 349 F. Supp. 866 (D.D.C. 1972).

In 1973 Congress enacted section 504 of the Rehabilitation Act of 1973. Section 504 prohibits recipients of federal financial assistance from discriminating against persons on the basis of their handicaps. The original legislation defined a handicapped person in terms of employment and ability to benefit from rehabilitation services. In 1974 Congress clarified its intent that section 504 was not limited to employment but rather covered all handicapped persons, including children and youth in relation to education.

In 1975 Congress passed the Education for All Handicapped Children Act (P.L. 94–142), amending the Education of the Handicapped Act (EHA). EHA, as amended, guarantees a free appropriate public education to every handicapped child in a state that accepts EHA funds. EHA includes a process approach for determining what constitutes an "appropriate" education.

The essentials of the process approach are that: (1) the determination of what a child's special educational needs are and what services will be provided must be based on the individual needs of that child; (2) parents and school district personnel have an equal interest and opportunity to participate in resolving the question of what is "appropriate" for the child; and (3) when parents and school districts disagree, there are fair procedures available to resolve differences, including due process hearings and reviews by the State educational agency.

In 1976, Congress adopted 42 U.S.C. 1988, which authorizes a court, at its discretion, to award reasonable attorneys' fees under, among other statutes, 42 U.S.C. 1983 to a party prevailing in any action or proceeding claiming abridgement of his/her constitutional rights.

In 1977 the Department of Health, Education, and Welfare issued regulations implementing section 504 and EHA. The Section 504 regulations were published in the *Federal Register* on May 4, 1977 and the regulations implementing Part B of EHA were published on August 23, 1977. Each regulation recognized the existence of the other and in explaining the relationship between the two each recognized that Congress intended that the other law constituted a separate but equally viable statement of the rights of handicapped children and youth to a free appropriate public education.

Section 504 is enforced by the Office for Civil Rights and EHA Is administered by the Office of Special Education Programs (SEP), formerly the Bureau of Education for the Handicapped (BEH).

In 1978, Congress amended title V of the Rehabilitation Act of 1973 to include a new section (section 505) that provides reasonable attorneys' fees to the prevailing party in any action or proceeding brought under section 504.

In sum, since 1978, it has been Congress' intent to permit parents or guardians to pursue the rights of handicapped children through EHA, section 504, and section 1983. Attorneys' fees could be awarded under section 504 (by virtue of section 5) and under section 1983 (by virtue of section 1988). Further, Congress, by establishing a comprehensive scheme of procedural protections under EHA (see above) expected that in appropriate situations these procedures would be used before a parent or guardian filed a law suit.

Congressional intent was ignored by the U.S. Supreme Court when, on July 5, 1984, it handed down its decision in Smith v. Robinson, 468 U.S. 992 (1984). . . .

H.R. 1523 is designed to: (1) authorize courts to award reasonable attorneys' fees to parents of handicapped children who prevail in actions or proceedings under EHA; (2) re-establish statutory rights repealed by the U.S. Supreme Court in *Smith v. Robinson*; (3) reaffirm, in light of this decision, the viability of section 504, 42 U.S.C. 1983, and other statutes as separate vehicles for ensuring the rights of handicapped children, and the role of OCR in investigating complaints of handicapped discrimination under section 504; and (4) improve the due process procedures available to handicapped children under EHA.

AWARD OF ATTORNEYS' FEES

Section 2 of the bill amends section 615(e)(4) of EHA to permit a court, in its discretion, to award reasonable attorneys' fees, costs, and expenses to the parents or guardian of a handicapped child or youth who is the prevailing party in an action or proceeding (a due process hearing or a state level review) brought under Part B of EHA.

The "action or proceeding" language in section 2 of the bill is identical to the language in title VII of the Civil Rights Act of 1964, interpreted by the Supreme Court in New York Gaslight Club v. Carey, 447 U.S. 54 (1980). In *Gaslight,* the Court held that the use of the phrase "action or proceeding" indicates an intent to subject the losing party to an award of attorneys' fees, expenses and costs incurred in court. The Court's decision also established a similar right under title VII to obtain an award of fees, costs, and expenses incurred in mandatory state and local administrative proceedings, even where no lawsuit is filed.

Consistent with the Supreme Court's reasoning in *Gaslight,* since EHA, like title VII, requires parents to exhaust administrative remedies before seeking judicial relief, if a parent loses at the local or state administrative proceeding but wins on appeal in federal court, the court may award reasonable fees for services performed in connection with both the administrative proceedings and the civil action.

Further, if a parent prevails on the merits at an administrative proceeding (and the agency does not appeal the decision), the parent may be awarded reasonable attorneys' fees, costs, and expenses incurred in such administrative proceeding. Usually, the amount of such fees, costs, and expenses will be agreed to by the public agency. If no agreement is possible, the parent may file a law suit for the limited purpose of receiving an award of reasonable fees, costs, and expenses.

By adopting the "action or proceeding" language, the Committee is guaranteeing that handicapped children and youth and their families are receiving the same protections which the Congress has extended to all other groups (such as minorities and women) in civil rights laws providing for attorneys' fees. By adopting the "action or proceeding" language, the Committee is also increasing the possibility that poor parents will have access to the procedural rights in EHA, thereby making the laws' protections available to all.

It is the Committee's intent that the terms "prevailing party" and "reasonable" be construed consistent with the U.S. Supreme Court's decision in Hensley v. Eckerhart, 461 U.S. 424, 103 S.Ct. 1933 (1983).

The phrase "expenses and costs" includes expenses of expert witnesses; the reasonable costs of any study, report, test, or project which is found to be necessary for the preparation of the parents' or guardian's due process hearing, state administrative review or civil action; as well as traditional costs and expenses incurred in the course of litigating a case (*e.g.,* depositions and interrogatories).

It is also the Committee's intent that, consistent with section 300.10 of title 34 (EHA regulations), the term "parent" includes a person acting as a parent of a child or a surrogate parent who has been appointed in accordance with section 615(b)(1)(B) of EHA. The term does not include the State if the child is the ward of the State. Of course, under appropriate circumstances a child or youth may also bring an action or proceeding under EHA and receive an award of attorney's fees to the extent he/she prevails.

SUMMARY

The Committee on Education and Labor finds that H.R. 1523, as amended appropriately authorizes the award of reasonable attorneys' fees to parents who are prevailing parties; clarifies the effect of the Education of the Handicapped Act on rights, procedures, and remedies under section 504 of the Rehabilitation Act of 1973 and other laws redressing the rights of handicapped children; and otherwise amends part B of EHA.

SECTION-BY-SECTION ANALYSIS

SHORT TITLE

Section 1 of the bill cites the title as the "Handicapped Children's Protection Act of 1985".

AWARD OF ATTORNEYS' FEES

Section 2 of the bill amends section 615(e)(4) of the Education of Handicapped Act (EHA) to authorize the court, at its discretion to award reasonable attorneys' fees, costs, and expenses to a parent who prevails in an action or proceeding brought under such section. Section 2 also specifies that fee awards should be based on the prevailing community rates for the kind and quality of services furnished and prohibits the use of EHA funds to pay the fees, costs and expenses awarded.

EFFECT OF EDUCATION OF THE HANDICAPPED
ACT ON OTHER LAWS

Section 3(a) of the bill amends section 615 of EHA by requiring handicapped children and youth to exhaust administrative remedies set out in part B of EHA before filing a law suit under section 504 of the Rehabilitation Act of 1973 or other federal laws redressing the rights of handicapped children and youth where relief also available under EHA.

Section 3(b) of the bill provides that with respect to preschool, elementary. secondary, and adult education programs and activities section 504 of the Rehabilitation Act of 1973 shall be carried out in accordance with regulations under such section in effect on July 4, 1984, unless expressly authorized by Act or Joint Resolution of the Congress approved after July 4, 1984.

IMPROVEMENTS IN PROCEDURAL SAFEGUARDS UNDER THE ACT

Section 4(a) of the bill amends section 615(d)(4) of EHA by specifying that local and state hearing decisions must be made available to the public without breaching the privacy rights of the handicapped children involved in the hearings.

Section 4(b) of the bill amends section 615(b)(2) of EHA to require public agencies to meet informally with parents in an attempt to resolve complaints informally before proceeding to a due process hearing. Any decision regarding participation in an informal meeting may not affect the availability or provision of any rights of the parents or guardian.

Section 4(c) prohibits a person (such as an employee or official of a State educational agency, local educational agency or intermediate educational unit) from, among other things, retaliating against a person because such person exercised certain rights in a meeting, hearing, review, investigation, or other activity related to the administration of, exercise of, authority under, or right secured by part B of EHA.

EFFECTIVE DATE

Section 5 of the bill specifies the effective date of the bill as the date of enactment, except that sections 2 and 3 apply with respect to actions or proceedings brought under section 615(e) of the EHA after July 3, 1984 and actions or proceedings brought prior to July 4 1984, under such sections which were pending on July 4, 1984.

SUPPLEMENTAL VIEWS (H.R. 1523), THE HANDICAPPED
CHILDREN'S PROTECTION ACT OF 1985

. . . We support the major objective of H.R. 1523 which appropriately responds to *Smith* by amending P.L. 94–142 to allow Courts to authorize an award of reasonable attorneys' fees to parents who prevail in P.L. 94–142 court actions.

Unwisely, H.R. 1523 extends, without limitation, the right to recover attorneys' fees to the administrative procedures available under P.L. 94–142 for the first time. This provision could radically alter the delicate balance that currently exists in P.L. 94–142's due process system, resulting in a severe financial burden for state educational agencies and local school systems. . . . H.R. 1523, by allowing for the recovery by a prevailing parent of attorneys' fees at the administrative level without limitation, invites the use of attorneys into a proceeding which does not require either party to be represented by counsel. The increased participation of attorneys in these procedures will lead to a more adversarial relationship between parents and educators and force school systems to use their precious educational dollars to pay lawyers whose participation is not only not required by law, but also may prove counterproductive. In effect, the Federal government, which presently contributes approximately 8 percent of the cost of educating a handicapped child, would, under H.R. 1523, require state education agencies and local school systems to spend their educational funds . . . to pay attorneys' fees in a Federally mandated administrative hearing system in those instances when the state and local educational agencies were carrying out their public responsibility of providing what they considered to be an appropriate education.

As voted unanimously out of the Subcommittee on Select Education, H.R. 1523 contained provisions which set certain limitations on fees at the administrative level and represented a bipartisan compromise. To the chagrin of Members who had forged this agreement, a substitute version of H.R. 1523 was introduced at the Full Committee, containing the current controversial provision on fees at the administrative level. Members of the Subcommittee who had marked-up and unanimously passed out of Subcommittee a bill in April of 1985 were confronted in September, 1985, with a radically different substitute bill at the Full Committee, without explanation or benefit to consider the new provision as a Subcommittee.

A second major concern with HR. 1523 is the provision which "codifies" the regulations under Section 504 of the Rehabilitation Act of 1973. H.R. 1523 will freeze the Section 504 regulations in effect on July 4, 1984, prohibiting the Executive Branch from proposing changes in the regulations unless expressly authorized by an Act or Joint Resolution of the Congress. That provision goes far beyond any action needed to respond to *Smith,* is overly broad in scope, could be read to cover current regulations of many agencies in addition to the Department of Education (including the Departments of Agriculture, Health and Human Services, and Interior, as well as the National Science Foundation and the Veterans' Administration), and is not based on careful consideration of each affected provision.

This codification is an intrusion into the authority of the Executive Branch to administer an important civil rights statute, and ties the hands of any Administration to deal effectively with a dynamic area of law.

... The failure of the Committee on Education and Labor to demonstrate reasonable restraint on this legislation should not be repeated by the House. We encourage Members to support efforts that will address these issues.

> JIM JEFFORDS.
>
> BILL GOODLING.
>
> THOMAS E. PETRIL.
>
> MARGE ROUKEMA.
>
> STEVE GUNDERSON.
>
> STEVE BARTLETT.
>
> ROD CHANDLER.
>
> TOM TAUKE.
>
> DICK ARMEY.

b. HOUSE DEBATES

131 Congressional Record (House of Representatives)

Tuesday, November 12, 1985
99th Cong. 1st Sess. 26 131 Cong. Rec. H9964

HANDICAPPED CHILDREN'S PROTECTION ACT OF 1985

Mr. WILLIAMS. . . .

Madam Speaker, on March 7, 1985, H.R. 1523, the Handicapped Children's Protection Act was introduced. The original bill was designed to accomplish four basic objectives.

> First, to authorize courts to award reasonable attorneys' fees to parents of handicapped children who prevail in specified circumstances under Part B of the Education of the Handicapped Act.
>
> Second, to reestablish statutory rights repealed by the U.S. Supreme Court in the decision in Smith versus Robinson.
>
> Third, to reaffirm, in light of this decision, the viability of section 504 of the Rehabilitation Act of 1973, 42 U.S.C. 1983 and other statutes as separate vehicles for ensuring the rights of handicapped children.
>
> Fourth, to improve the due process procedures available under part B of the Education of the Handicapped Act.

Today, we are considering an amendment in the nature of a substitute which satisfies all of these objectives. The road traveled to reach this bipartisan compromise has not been smooth. The issues involved in the legislation are extremely complex and affect all participants in our educational system: Handicapped children and their families, teachers, and school officials. However, Members on both sides of the aisle have worked long and hard to reach this bipartisan compromise. Special recognition must go to Mr. Hawkins, Mr. Biaggi, Mr. Jeffords, and Mr. Bartlett. My personal thanks for all your efforts.

In the course of drafting this legislation, organizations representing handicapped children, parents, educators, administrators, boards of education have often expressed strong and often divergent positions on the provisions in the bill. The consequences of including or excluding particular provisions were expressed and then debated at length.

The bill we present today for passage represents a consensus which achieves the needed balance between the rights of handicapped children and local and State educational agencies. I urge my colleagues to support this bipartisan substitute.

Let me briefly describe the key components of the legislation.

First, it amends part B of EHA to provide that a parent or guardian of a handicapped child who prevails against a school district or State educational agency in a civil action in Federal or State court, or an administrative proceeding such as a due process hearing or State appeal, may be awarded reasonable attorney's fees, costs and expenses by the court.

Second, it provides for the submission to Congress of a GAO study on the impact of this provision no later than 3 ½ years after the date of enactment of the legislation.

Third, the legislation contains a sunset provision under which a court's authority to award fees to parents who prevail in administrative proceedings terminates 4 years after the date of enactment of this legislation if the GAO report is submitted on schedule: Thus, after 4 years, unless Congress passes additional legislation, a court's authority to award fees will be limited to civil actions in State or Federal courts in which parents prevail.

Fourth, it overturns the U.S. Supreme Court's decision in Smith versus Robinson by reestablishing the viability of Section 504 of the Rehabilitation Act of 1973 and other statutes as separate vehicles for ensuring the rights of handicapped children and youth.

Fifth, it deletes section 3(b) of H.R. 1523, as reported out of the Education and Labor Committee. Section 3(b) provides that with respect to preschool, elementary, secondary, and adult education programs and activities, section 504 must continue to be carried out in accordance with the regulations in effect on July 4, 1984, unless expressly authorized by act or joint resolution of the Congress approved after July 4, 1984.

The decision to delete this provision from the bipartisan substitute should not be construed as reflecting Congressional change in support for the validity of the current section 504 regulations.

Sixth, the bipartisan substitute amends part B of the Education of the Handicapped Act to improve procedural protections under the act.

These changes include: a requirement that hearing decisions be made available to the public without diminishing the privacy rights of the children; a requirement that a school district provide a parent with an opportunity to meet informally with agency officials to resolve complaints prior to the due process hearings; and an anti-retaliation provision barring public agencies from taking adverse actions against persons participating or involved in, among other things, meetings or hearings.

Finally, the bill specifies that the provisions concerning the awarding of attorneys fees and the effect of the Education of the Handicapped Act on other laws apply retroactively with respect to actions or proceedings after July 3, 1984, and actions or proceedings brought prior to July 4, 1984, which were pending on July 4, 1984.

The Congressional Budget Office states that there will be no increase in Federal cost as a result of this bill.

Public Law 94–142 was hailed upon passage as a significant step forward in ensuring the educational rights of persons with handicaps and it is living up to its promises. This legislation before you today only strengthens that capability. I urge my colleagues to support the compromise.

Madam Speaker, I reserve the balance of my time.

The SPEAKER pro tempore. (Mr. Garcia). The Chair recognizes the gentleman from Texas [Mr. Bartlett].

Mr. BARTLETT. Mr. Speaker, I yield myself 14 ½ minutes.

(Mr. BARTLETT asked and was given permission to revise and extend his remarks.)

Mr. BARTLETT. . . .

Mr. Speaker, H.R. 1523 constructively addresses the issue of the recovery of attorneys' fees for civil action under Public Law 94–142 in response to the Smith decision. It properly authorizes courts to award reasonable attorneys' fees to parents of handicapped children who prevail in civil actions. I support without reservation, this portion of H.R. 1523, believing that not only the families of handicapped children will be served by this amendment but also the public interest of ensuring the provision of a free and appropriate education for all handicapped children.

Saying this, Mr. Speaker, I must raise what I consider to be a serious flaw in H.R. 1523 which taints its contributions to Public Law 94–142. H.R. 1523 mistakenly extends the authority for the recovery of attorneys' fees into Public Law 94–142's administrative hearing process. Public Law 94–142 is essentially a grant-in-aid statute that provides an informal process by which parents and educators can mutually determine what is an appropriate education for a handicapped student. The system for identifying, evaluating, developing, and administering the individualized educational program rests upon the ability of parents and educators to meet, share information, and agree upon a program.

When parents and educators disagree on what is educationally appropriate for a handicapped child, either party may file a request for an administrative hearing presided over by an impartial due process hearing officer. These hearing officers are trained by the State and are generally individuals with experience in special education or special education legal policy. The hearing officers are not required to be attorneys, and neither the parents nor the school systems are required to be represented by attorneys. The hearing officer's responsibility is to determine the appropriate education for the handicapped student based upon the information that the parents and the educators present.

Under H.R. 1523, for the first time, parents who retain an attorney for work conducted at the administrative hearing level will be able to recover fees if they prevail at the hearing, even if the issue does not go to court. This represents a significant departure from past and current practice, where it has only been the case four times since 1975 that courts have awarded attorneys' fees at the administrative level to parents who later prevailed in court action and never awarded attorneys' fees at the administrative level in cases which do not go on to court.

There are a number of very good reasons why this provision is both unnecessary and could be destructive. Foremost is an indisputable fact that the number of administrative hearings held each year to resolve disputes between parents and educators is decreasing. According to a survey by the National Association of State Directors of Special Education the number of first-level hearings decreased by 39 percent between 1979–80 and 1983–84. For the school year 1983–84 only 1 out of every 3,000 of the approximately 4 million students was involved in a first-level hearing and only 1 in every 64,800 was the subject of litigation.

Mr. Speaker, H.R. 1523 threatens to significantly alter a system of conflict resolution which is working as Congress intended, and no compelling evidence exists which supports a need to make this fundamental change. I am confident that Public Law 94–142's administrative hearing system is working fairly and properly, and I attribute this to its formal and inexpensive nature. My position is affirmed by the Rand study, and I quote:

> The administrative due process system offers plaintiffs the same kinds of protections and results as the courts, but at greater speed and lower cost. Parents and school officials are therefore generally eager to settle their disputes informally or in the administrative due process system.

H.R. 1523, by allowing for the recovery of fees at the administrative level, removes the incentive to resolve disputes informally because schools will be as liable for attorneys' fees under the administrative system as they are in court. The complications resulting from this part of

H.R. 1523 become even clearer when one considers the impact of fees at the administrative level on the mediation or informal complaint procedure that is also part of H. R. 1523.

The principle that I advocate on this issue is a simple one: Congress should not do anything to encourage the participation of lawyers in a conflict resolution situation which does not require their participation. By allowing for the recovery of attorneys' fees under Public Law 94–142 at the administrative level, H.R. 1523 will increase the participation of attorneys and decrease the likelihood that parents and educators will resolve their disputes informally and inexpensively.

I support H.R. 1523 at this time for two reasons: First, I do believe Congress should act to restore attorneys' fees to court level, and second, the bill includes sunset on the provision authorizing fees at the administrative level. This sunset will mean that after a sufficient period of time, Congress will be able to examine the impact of the bill as presently constituted and act accordingly. If this provision were not in H.R. 1523, I could not support the bill.

Mr. Speaker, H.R. 1523 serves a vital purpose of allowing courts to authorize attorneys' fees to parents who prevail in Public Law 94–142 litigation. H.R. 1523 also jeopardizes Public Law 94–142's administrative hearing system and the process by which parents and educators informally determine what is appropriate for a handicapped student.

Mr. Speaker, at this time, I would ask the gentleman from Montana [Mr. Williams] if he would engage in a colloquy.

Mr. WILLIAMS. Mr. Speaker, I will be pleased to join with my colleague in a colloquy.

Mr. BARTLETT. Mr. Speaker, section 2 of H.R. 1523 amends section 615(e)(4) of the Education of the Handicapped Act by adding the following new provision:

> In any action or proceeding brought under this subsection, the court, in its discretion, may award reasonable attorneys' fees, expenses, and costs to the parents or guardian of a handicapped child or youth who is the prevailing party.

Could you clarify the meaning of the terms "action" and "proceeding?"

Mr. WILLIAMS. The term "action" is intended to include a civil action filed in a State or Federal court. The term "proceeding" is limited to the due process hearing that parents are required to exhaust under 615(b)(2) and the State appeal under section 615(c). The term "proceeding" is not intended to include meetings held to develop individualized education programs or meetings to make decisions concerning such matters as the identification, evaluation, or placement of handicapped children.

Mr. BARTLETT. It is my understanding that parents are not entitled to any fees, costs, or expenses when they are declared the prevailing party in any action or proceeding but at the final appeal of such action or proceeding the school district is declared the prevailing party. Do you agree with this statement?

Mr. WILLIAMS. Yes, I do agree with that.

Mr. BARTLETT. Similarly, where the parents lose in any action or proceeding but at the final appeal of such action or proceeding the parents are declared the prevailing party, do you agree that they are entitled to reasonable fees, costs, and expenses related to all prior actions and proceedings as well as the final appeal?

Mr. WILLIAMS. Yes, I do.

Mr. BARTLETT. Would you clarify the meaning of the terms "reasonable" and "prevailing?"

Mr. WILLIAMS. These terms are intended to be construed as being consistent with all of the standards set forth in the U.S. Supreme Court's decision in HENSLEY V. ECKERHART, 461 U.S. 424 (1983).

The part of the bill that the gentleman from Texas says is flawed I regard as its strength. What we are talking about is providing attorneys' fees for those individuals who are being denied access to the educational system; access as provided by Public Law 94–142.

It is argued that the hearings are informal and that the school boards are generally cooperative. The reality of the matter is this: We are talking about Mr. or Mrs. John Doe who have a problem with a child gaining access, who then come before a school board. While most of us have experience, testifying in one forum or another; so hence we are not impressed nor more intimidated by a school board. Do we fully understand the psychological impact and burden it places on the parents appearing before a quasi-judicial body? There is an inhibition placed; they do not have the ability nor experience to argue and to make their case.

At the same time, the school board has present, on staff, their own attorneys; but absent that, members of the school board are not burdened with the same lack of experience. They have been subjected to election; they have been through the process time and time again; they come in an adversarial position, and that is the critical nature of this legislation and of this situation.

They are there to say that the child should not be in the school. The parents want the child in the program. So clearly, confrontation exists. It is important to establish a record, whether the parents prevail at this point or not, the record must be established. Most parents, by themselves, cannot effectively establish the record on which a step forward into the courts can be based. They do not have that knowledge or skills.

For the most part, they will not prevail, and oftentimes when they are rejected at that point, they leave and give up the fight, to the detriment of the child.

Mr. BARTLETT. Mr. Speaker, I yield 4 minutes to the gentleman from Vermont [Mr. Jeffords], the ranking member of the Education and Labor Committee.

(Mr. JEFFORDS asked and was given permission to revise and extend his remarks.)

Mr. JEFFORDS. Mr. Speaker, the bill before us today, H.R. 1523, the Handicapped Children's Protection Act, is necessary because of a Supreme Court decision in the case of Smith versus Robinson. There is no doubt that there is agreement among all of us that the decision rendered by the court in July 1984 must be overturned. . . . I must congratulate the chairman of the subcommittee, Mr. Williams, and the ranking Republican, Mr. Bartlett, for their efforts on this bill. The results of their labors is a bill that continues to support a handicapped child's rights, and the enforcement of those rights, to an appropriate education.

Currently there is no prohibition against the use of an attorney by either party at the administrative proceedings level. Neither the school district nor the parent is prohibited from using an attorney if so desired. Similarly, because one party has an attorney does not automatically trigger the requirement that the other party retain an attorney. We know though, that many school systems are understandably reluctant to hire attorneys. In a recent survey, 56 percent of the school districts questioned either never use an attorney, or only use one when the parent does. Our action in this bill may draw in the use of an attorney at an earlier stage in the proceedings than has been the norm to date. In this way, we may be disrupting a system of proven effectiveness. We may be providing a disincentive to resolve disagreements informally, as soon in the process as possible. We may instead be providing incentive to take the dispute to court.

The seriousness of this issue deserves discussion by this body. Our debate on the issue though, has been precluded somewhat by the action taken by the other body. Instead, concerns regarding the wisdom of providing for attorneys' fees at the administrative proceedings level have been partially addressed in H.R. 523 by the inclusion of a sunset provision. I appreciate the willingness of the majority to work with the minority on this point. By including a 4-year sunset provision directed toward the payment of attorney's fees at the hearing level, and requiring a GAO study to assess the effects of the provision, we can review the outcome and make the appropriate changes if they are necessary. I hope that my fears are proven wrong. It would be nice to be able to come to this body 4 years from now and heartily endorse the payment of attorneys' fees at the administrative level. I am not sure that such an action will be supported by our findings.

None of us disputes the intent of this bill. We all want to see the decision in Smith versus Robinson overturned, and allow the courts to authorize the payment of attorneys' fees to parents who prevail in Public Law 94–142 litigation. We may have tipped the scales too far in favor of such payments, but I believe that the balance we seek comes through the sunset provision added by the committee amendments today.

All children have the right to a free and appropriate education. Parents have the right to protect the rights of their children in this regard. We must act to retain these rights. These efforts should be supported and I encourage my colleagues to do so.

The SPEAKER pro tempore. The question is on the motion offered by the gentleman from Montana [Mr. Williams] that the House suspend the rules and pass the bill, H.R. 1523, as amended.

The question was taken; and (two-thirds having voted in favor thereof) the rules were suspended, and the bill, as amended, was passed.

A motion to reconsider was laid on the table.

[At this point, following an established House procedure, the text of H.R. 1523 was substituted for that of S. 415, and S. 415 as thus amended, was approved. S. 415, as passed by the House, thus contained the language of H.R. 1523.]

APPOINTMENT OF CONFEREES ON S. 415

Mr. WILLIAMS. Mr. Speaker, I ask unanimous consent that the House insist on its amendment to the Senate bill, S. 415, and request a conference with the Senate thereon.

The SPEAKER pro tempore. Is there objection to the request of the gentleman from Montana? The Chair hears none and, without objection, appoints the following conferees: Messrs. Hawkins, Biaggi, Williams, Hayes, Martinez, Eckart of Ohio, Jeffords, Goodling, Coleman of Missouri, and Bartlett.

There was no objection.

IV. CONFERENCE REPORT

House and Senate representatives met and resolved their differences, as reported below. Pay close attention to what were, and what were not, controversial issues requiring compromise.

a. REPORT

99TH CONGRESS 2nd Session	HOUSE OF REPRESENTATIVES	REPORT 99–687

Handicapped Children's Protection Act of 1986

JULY 16, 1986.—Ordered to be printed

Mr. HAWKINS, from the committee of conference, submitted the following

CONFERENCE REPORT [To accompany S. 415]

The committee of conference on the disagreeing votes of the two Houses on the amendments of the House to the bill (S. 415), to amend the Education of the Handicapped Act to authorize the award of reasonable attorneys' fees to certain prevailing parties, and to clarify the effect of the Education of the Handicapped Act on rights, procedures, and remedies under other laws relating to the prohibition of discrimination, having met, after full and free conference, have agreed to recommend and do recommend to their respective Houses as follows:

That the Senate recede from its disagreement to the amendment of the House to the text of the bill and agree to the same with an amendment as follows:

In lieu of the matter proposed to be inserted by the House amendment, insert the following:

SHORT TITLE

SECTION 1. This Act may be cited as the "Handicapped Children's Protection Act of 1986".

AWARD OF ATTORNEYS' FEES

SEC. 2. Section 615(e)(4) of the Education of the Handicapped Act is amended by inserting "(A)" after the paragraph designation and by adding at the end thereof the following new subparagraphs:

"(B) In any action or proceeding brought under this subsection, the court, in its discretion, may award reasonable attorneys' fees as part of the costs to the parents or guardian of a handicapped child or youth who is the prevailing party.

"(C) For the purpose of this subsection, fees awarded under this subsection shall be based on rates prevailing in the community in which the action or proceeding arose for the kind and quality of services furnished. No bonus or multiplier may be used in calculating the fees awarded under this subsection.

"(D) No award of attorneys' fees and related costs may be made in any action or proceeding under this subsection for services performed subsequent to the time of a written offer of settlement to a parent or guardian, if—

"i) the offer is made within the time prescribed by Rule 68 of the Federal Rules of Civil Procedure or, in the case of an administrative proceeding, at any time more than ten days before the proceeding begins;

"ii) the offer is not accepted within ten days; and

"iii) the court or administrative officer finds that the relief finally obtained by the parents or guardian is not more favorable to the parents or guardian than the offer of settlement.

"(E) Notwithstanding the provisions of subparagraph (D), an award of attorneys' fees and related costs may be made to a parent or guardian who is the prevailing party and who was substantially justified in rejecting the settlement offer.

"(F) Whenever the court finds that—

"i) the parent or guardian, during the course of the action or proceeding, unreasonably protracted the final resolution of the controversy;

"ii) the amount of the attorneys' fees otherwise authorized to be awarded unreasonably exceeds the hourly rate prevailing in the community for similar services by attorneys of reasonably comparable skill, experience, and reputation; or

"iii) the time spent and legal services furnished were excessive considering the nature of the action or proceeding

the court shall reduce, accordingly, the amount of the attorneys' fees awarded under this subsection.

"(G) The provisions of subparagraph (F) shall not apply in any action or proceeding if the court finds that the State or local educational agency unreasonably protracted the final resolution of the action or proceeding or there was a violation of section 615 of this Act.".

EFFECT OF EDUCATION OF THE HANDICAPPED ACT ON OTHER LAWS

SEC. 3.   Section 615 of the Education of the Handicapped Act is amended by adding at the end thereof the following new subsection.

"(f) Nothing in this title shall be construed to restrict or limit the rights, procedures, and remedies available under the Constitution, title

V of the Rehabilitation Act of 1973, or other Federal statutes protecting the rights of handicapped children and youth, except that before the filing of a civil action under such laws seeking relief that is also available under this part, the procedures under subsections (b)(2) and (c) shall be exhausted to the same extent as would be required had the action been brought under this part."

GAO STUDY OF ATTORNEYS' FEES PROVISION

SEC. 4.   (a) The Comptroller General of the United States, through the General Accounting Office, shall conduct a study of the impact of the amendments to the Education of the Handicapped Act made under section 2 of this Act. Not later than June 30, 1989, the Comptroller General shall submit a report containing the findings of such study to the Committee on Education and Labor of the House of Representatives and the Committee on Labor and Human Resources of the Senate. The Comptroller General shall conduct a formal briefing for such Committees on the status of the study not later than March 1, 1988. Such report shall include the information described in subsection (b).

(b) The report authorized under subsection (a) shall include the following information:

(1) The number, in the aggregate and by State, of written decisions under section 615 (b)(2) and (c) transmitted to State advisory panels under section 615(d)(4) for fiscal years 1984 through 1988, the prevailing party in each such decision, and the type of complaint. For fiscal year 1986, the report shall designate which decisions concern complaints filed after the date of the enactment of this Act.

(2) the number, in the aggregate and by State, of civil actions brought under section 615(e)(2), the prevailing party in each action, and the type of complaint for fiscal years 1984 through 1988. For fiscal year 1986 the report shall designate which decisions concern complaints filed after the date of enactment.

(3) Data, for a geographically representative selective sample of states, indicating (A) the specific amount of attorneys' fees, costs, and expenses awarded to the prevailing party, in each action and proceeding under section 615(e)(4)(B) from the date of the enactment of this Act through fiscal year 1988, and the range of such fees, costs, and expenses awarded in the actions and proceedings under such section, categorized by type of complaint and (B) for the same sample as in (A) the number of hours spent by personnel, including attorneys and consultants, involved in the action or proceeding, and expenses incurred by the parents and the State educational agency and local educational agency.

(4) Data, for a geographically representative sample of States, on the experience of educational agencies in resolving complaints informally under section 615(b)(2), from the date of the enactment of this Act through fiscal year 1988.

EFFECTIVE DATE

SEC. 5.   The amendment made by section 2 shall apply with respect to actions or proceedings brought under section 615(e) of the Education of the Handicapped Act after July 3, 1984, and actions or proceedings brought prior to July 4, 1984, under such section which was pending on July 4, 1984.

And the House agree to the same.

That the Senate recede from its disagreement to the amendment of the House to the title of the bill, and agree to the same.

AUGUSTUS F. HAWKINS,

MARIO BIAGGI,

PAT WILLIAMS,

CHARLES A. HAYES,

MATTHEW H. MARTINEZ,

DENNIS E. ECKART,

Managers on the Part of the House.

ORRIN HATCH,

LOWELL. P. WEICKER, JR.,

DON NICKLES,

TED KENNEDY,

JOHN F. KERRY,

Managers on the Part of the Senate.

JOINT EXPLANATORY STATEMENT OF THE COMMITTEE OF CONFERENCE

The managers on the part of the House and the Senate at the conference on the disagreeing votes of the two Houses on the amendment of the House to the bill (S. 415) to authorize the award of attorneys' fees to certain prevailing parties, and to clarify the effect of the Education of the Handicapped Act on rights, procedures and remedies under other laws relating to the prohibition of discrimination and for other purposes, submit the following joint statement to the House and the Senate in explanation of the effect of the action agreed upon by the managers and recommended in the accompanying conference report. The differences between the Senate bill and the House amendment and the substitute agreed to at the conference, are noted below, except for clerical corrections, conforming changes made necessary by agreements reached by the conferees, and minor drafting and clarifying changes.

The Senate bill provides for "a reasonable attorney's fee."

The House amendment provides for "reasonable attorneys' fees." The Senate recedes.

With slightly different wording, both the Senate bill and the House amendment provide for the awarding of attorneys' fees in addition to costs.

The Senate recedes to the House and the House recedes to the Senate with an amendment clarifying that "the court, in its discretion, may award reasonable attorneys' fees as part of the costs. . . ." This change in wording incorporates the Supreme Court Marek v. Chesny decision (473 U.S. 1, 87 L.Ed.2d 1).

The conferees intend that the term "attorneys' fees as part of the costs" include reasonable expenses and fees of expert witnesses and reasonable costs of any test or evaluation which is found to be necessary for the preparation of the parent or guardian's case in the action or proceeding, as well as traditional costs incurred in the course of litigating a case.

The Senate bill provides for the award of attorney's fees "to a parent or legal representative."

The House amendment provides for the award of attorneys' fees "to the parents or guardian."

The Senate recedes.

The Senate bill limits the amount of the fee awarded whenever a parent or legal representative is represented by a publicly funded organization which provides legal services.

The House amendment provides that fee awards shall be based on prevailing rates in the community.

The House recedes to the Senate and the Senate recedes to the House with an amendment clarifying that "fees awarded under this subsection shall be based on rates prevailing in the community in which the action or proceeding arose for the kind and quality of the services furnished." See, Hensley v. Eckerhart, 461 U.S. 424 (1983); Marek v. Chesny, 473 U.S. 1, 87 L.Ed.2d 1 (1985); and Blum v. Stenson, 465 U.S. 886, 104 S.Ct. 1541 (1984). However, no such awards of attorneys' fees shall be calculated by using bonuses or multipliers. The conferees want to make it clear that the inclusion of the prohibition against calculation of fees using bonuses and multipliers is limited to cases brought only under part B of the Education of the Handicapped Act. The conferees do not intend in any way to diminish the applicability of interpretation by the U.S. Supreme Court regarding bonuses and multipliers to other statutes such as 42 U.S.C. 1988. See, Hensley v. Eckerhart, Blum v. Stenson, Evans v. Jeff D., 475 U.S. 717, 106 S.Ct. 1531 (1986). In addition, several new sections would be added to clarify that under part B of the Education of the Handicapped Act, no award of attorneys' fees and related costs subject to the provision of the act may be made for services performed subsequent to the time a written offer of settlement is made to a party (if the offer is made at least 10 days prior to the date of the action or proceeding) if the offer is not accepted within ten days and a court or administrative officer finds that the relief finally obtained by the party is not more favorable to the parent or guardian than the offer of settlement. However, attorneys' fees may be awarded to a prevailing parent or guardian who was substantially justified in rejecting the settlement offer. Furthermore, the court shall reduce accordingly the amount of attorneys' fees and related expenses otherwise allowable if they determine that:

(1) the parent or guardian, during the course of the action or proceeding unreasonably protracted the final resolution of the controversy;

(2) the amount of attorneys' fees otherwise authorized to be awarded unreasonably exceeds the hourly rate prevailing in the community for similar services by attorneys of reasonably comparable skills experience and reputation; or

(3) the time spent and legal services furnished were excessive considering the nature of the action or proceeding.

Finally, the preceding situations in which the court reduces the amount of fees and related expenses otherwise allowable shall not apply if the local or state educational agency is determined to have unreasonably protracted the final resolution of the action or proceeding or if a violation of section 615 of the Education of the Handicapped Act is found.

The conferees intend that this provision clarify the application of the Marek v. Chesny decision to the Handicapped Children's Protection Act. One exception is made to the applicability of the Marek v. Chesny decision. When the parent or guardian is substantially justified in rejecting the settlement offer, the Marek v. Chesny decision would not apply. Substantial justification for rejection would include relevant pending court decisions which could have an impact on the case in question.

In enumerating three conditions under which the amount of attorneys' fees would be reduced, the committee intends to protect against excessive reimbursement. The second condition is a codification of the policy for awarding fees in footnote 11 of Blum v. Stenson.

5.   The House amendment, but not the Senate bill, specifies that fees, expenses, and costs awarded to the prevailing party may not be paid with the funds provided under part B of EHA. The report accompanying the Senate's bill restates existing policy that bars the payment of such fees and the costs under part B.

The House recedes. The conferees wish to emphasize that existing law bars payment of attorneys' fees with funds appropriated under B of EHA.

6.   The House amendment, but not the Senate bill, provides for a GAO study of the impact of the bill authorizing the awarding of fees and costs.

The Senate recedes to the House with an amendment expanding the data collection requirements of the GAO study to include information regarding the amount of funds expended by local educational agencies and state educational agencies on civil actions and administrative proceedings.

7.   The House amendment, but not the Senate bill, sunsets the court's authority to award fees at the administrative level after a period of time specified in the legislation.

The House recedes.

8.   With slightly different wording, both the Senate bill and the House amendment authorize the filing of civil actions under legal authorities other than part B of EHA so long as parents first exhaust administrative remedies available under part B of EHA to the same extent as would be required under that part.

The House recedes. It is the conferees' intent that actions brought under 42 U.S.C. 1983 are governed by this provision.

9.   The House amendment, but not the Senate bill requires public access to hearing decisions.

The House recedes. The conferees wish to emphasize that public access to hearing decisions is existing law.

10.   The House amendment, but not the Senate bill, requires that the public educational agency provide parents with an opportunity to meet informally in an attempt to resolve a complaint.

The House recedes.

11.   The House amendment, but not the Senate bill, includes an anti-retaliation provision.

The House recedes. It is the conferees' intent that no person may discharge, intimidate, retaliate, threaten, coerce, or otherwise take an adverse action against any person because such person has filed a complaint, testified, furnished information, assisted or participated in any manner in a meeting, hearing, review, investigation, or other activity related to the administration of, exercise of authority under, or right secured by part B of EHA. The term "person" the first time it is used means a state educational agency, local educational agency, intermediate educational unit or any official or employee thereof.

11.   The House amendment, but not the Senate bill, makes retroactive its provision regarding the effect of EHA on other laws (section 3).

The House recedes.

AUGUSTUS F. HAWKINS,

MARIO BIAGGI,

PAT WILLIAMS,

CHARLES A. HAYES,

MATTHEW H. MARTINEZ,

DENNIS E. ECKART,

Managers on the Part of the House.

ORRIN HATCH,

LOWELL. P. WEICKER, JR.,

DON NICKLES,

TED KENNEDY,

JOHN F. KERRY,

Managers on the Part of the Senate.

b.   SENATE CONSIDERATION OF CONFERENCE REPORT

132 Congressional Record (Senate)

Thursday, July 17, 1986; (Legislative day of Monday, July 14, 1986)
99th Cong. 2nd Sess. 132 Cong. Rec. S. 9277

Mr. WEICKER. Mr. President, I rise in support of the conference report on S. 415, the Handicapped Children's Protection Act.

The Handicapped Children's Protection Act states explicitly what is implicit in the Education of the Handicapped Act regarding the civil right of handicapped children to an education. By allowing the courts to award attorneys' fees to prevailing parents or guardians, handicapped children are protected against discrimination in the same manner as are other vulnerable groups. What we do here today is to make the Education of the Handicapped Act consistent with more than 130 other fee shifting statutes which provide for the award of attorneys' fees to parties who prevail in court to obtain what is guaranteed to them by law. Without this remedy, many of our civil rights would be hollow pronouncements available only to those who could afford to sue for enforcement of their rights.

The passage of this bill today reaffirms our commitment to equality of opportunity and equal justice for all. Today, we stand together in our resolve to recognize the handicapped members of our society as citizens of this Nation—entitled to all rights and remedies available under the law.

Finally, I particularly want to thank my colleagues Senator Hatch, the chairman of the Committee on Labor and Human Resources; and Senator Kerry, the ranking minority member of the Subcommittee on the

Handicapped, for their diligent efforts at accommodating diverse points of view in developing this conference agreement.

I urge the adoption of the conference report.

I yield to the distinguished Senator from Massachusetts, the ranking member of the Subcommittee on the Handicapped.

MR. KENNEDY: Mr. President, I rise in strong support of the pending conference report on S. 415, the Handicapped Children's Protection Act. This vital legislation reverses a U.S. Supreme Court decision Smith versus Robinson which has had a devastating effect on the ability of parents of handicapped children to fully access legal remedies available to them which protect their handicapped children's educational rights. The conference report concludes many weeks of dedicated work on the part of Members and their staff, resulting in an impressive initiative designed to enhance the opportunities for equality in education for persons with disabilities. In particular I would like to commend the subcommittee chairman, Senator Weicker and his staff for their excellent contribution to this piece of legislation. Senator Weicker's unbending commitment to uphold the rights of all handicapped individuals is a model for us to follow. I applaud his tireless efforts in this area.

This conference report represents a victory in protecting the educational rights of all handicapped children regardless of their economic situation. I commend my colleagues on the conference committee for eliminating a dangerous provision in the Senate-passed bill which placed a cap on attorneys' fees for publicly funded attorneys but did not set the same limitations on attorneys' fees for privately funded attorneys. By eliminating this blatant double standard and permitting attorneys' fees to reflect the prevailing rates in the community, the conferees have endorsed the concept that economically disadvantaged handicapped children will not be singled out and unfairly discriminated against. By removing the cap, the conferees have wisely recognized the fact that the lack of sufficient funding sources seriously impedes the ability of public advocates to adequately work on behalf of indigent handicapped children when their educational rights are being denied. . . .

By striking the cap, the conference report will encourage schools to settle cases expeditiously and will consequently deter reluctant schools from prolonging judicial proceedings in an attempt to force plaintiffs to abandon their case. The attorneys' fees cap greatly undermined the strength of this act and simply did a disservice to all disabled students and their families; once again I commend its elimination.

Mr. HATCH. Mr. President, today, we are considering the final passage of S. 415, the Handicapped Children's Protection Act of 1986. This legislation originally was introduced 3 years ago in response to the Smith versus Robinson Supreme Court decision. In order to clarify the intent of Congress and reaffirm the rights of handicapped children as provided under Public Law 94–142, Senator Weicker introduced S. 2859 which was later reintroduced at the beginning of the 99th Congress as S. 415. As cosponsor of S. 415 and as a conferee, I am pleased that the conference agreement we are now voting on reflects the culmination of several years of deliberation and refinement.

The agreement we are now considering is a compromise which I feel accomplishes two major objectives. First, it provides for the award of reasonable attorney's fees to prevailing parents in an Education of the Handicapped Act action or proceeding.

Second, it includes the application of provisions from the Marek versus Chesny, Blum versus Stenson, Evans versus Jeff D., and Henley versus Eckerhart decisions to cases brought under part B of the Education of the Handicapped Act in order to protect against excessive reimbursement.

Mr. WEICKER. Mr. President, I move adoption of the conference report.

The PRESIDING OFFICER. The question is on agreeing to the conference report.

The conference report was agreed to.

c.   HOUSE CONSIDERATION OF CONFERENCE REPORT

132 Congressional Record (House of Representatives)
Thursday, July 17, 1986; (Legislative day of Monday, July 14, 1986)
99th Cong. 2nd Sess. 132 Cong. Rec. H. 4841

Mr. WILLIAMS. Mr. Speaker, I call up the conference report on the Senate bill (S. 415) to amend the Education of the Handicapped Act to authorize the award of reasonable attorneys' fees to certain prevailing parties, and to clarify the effect of the Education of the Handicapped Act on rights, procedures, and remedies under other laws relating to the prohibition of discrimination.

Mr. Speaker, I rise in support of the conference report concerning S. 415 and H.R. 1523, the Handicapped Children's Protection Act of 1986. . . . The provisions in the conference report and the accompanying statement of managers are the result of protracted negotiations with the Senate conferees. We did not get everything we wanted and they didn't get everything they wanted. However, overall, I am pleased to report that the conference agreement contains most of the key provisions in the House bill and excludes the major provision in the Senate bill that was an anathema to the House.

Let me briefly describe the key provisions in the conference agreement.

First, with slightly different wording, both the Senate bill and the House amendment provide for the awarding of attorneys' fees in addition to costs to parents who prevail in any action or proceeding. Under the conference agreement, the Senate recedes to the House and the House recedes to the Senate with an amendment clarifying that the court in its discretion may award reasonable attorneys' fees to the prevailing parents as part of the costs of the action or proceeding.

The Senate conferees also agreed to accept, with certain minor changes, the provision in the House bill calling for a GAO study of the impact of section 2 of the bill.

The conference agreement does not include the "sunset provision" which was included in the House bill. Under this provision, the authority of the court to award fees to parents prevailing at administrative hearings would be repealed in 4 years. This provision was of particular concern to the House Republican conferees. On three separate occasions, all conferees from the other body rejected requests to include the "sunset" provision in the conference agreement.

Finally, the Senate agreed to include language in the statement of managers (taken verbatim from the House bill and report) that makes it clear that under current law, persons may not be retaliated against by public agencies for their actions relating to Public Law 94–142.

As Members know, the Congress has been working for many months on this legislation. Members and their staffs, on both sides of the aisle and in both bodies have been diligent in their efforts to resolve differences and put in place a solution that strikes the right balance of protections. I think we have succeeded. I especially want to express my appreciation to Gus Hawkins, Mario Biaggi, Jim Jeffords, and Steve Bartlett for the significant role they and their staffs have played on this legislation.

I urge my colleagues to support this important legislation. Public Law 94–142, the landmark legislation that recently celebrated its 10th anniversary, entitles every handicapped child to a free appropriate public education. If we are going to make this statutory right a reality for all, we must adopt the Handicapped Children's Protection Act conference report.

Mr. Speaker, I reserve the balance of my time.

Mr. JEFFORDS. Mr. Speaker, I yield such time as he may consume to the gentleman from Texas [Mr. Bartlett].

(Mr. BARTLETT asked and was given permission to revise and extend his remarks.)

Mr. BARTLETT. I thank the gentleman for yielding time to me.

Mr. Speaker, I support those provisions in the conference agreement that, in response to the Supreme Court decision in the case of Smith versus Robinson, authorizes the awarding of reasonable attorneys' fees to parents who prevail in special education court cases. Unfortunately, the conference agreement goes well beyond a reasonable congressional response to Smith versus Robinson, and places our special education's hearing system at risk of becoming litigious and increasingly adversarial.

This has been a difficult piece of legislation. It concerns a particularly volatile issue—namely, attorneys' fees. Attorneys' fees litigation and issues surrounding the recovery of fees are crowding our judicial system's dockets. This should be a red flag to Congress. In this legislation, we have wrestled with the issue of attorneys' fees in a sensitive area—the education of handicapped children. It has taken 2 years to write a three-page bill. The process has been trying, and there are many of us who have been involved in that process who are not entirely satisfied with this legislation, but who feel that its benefits outweigh its potential limitations.

This conference agreement contains a number of desirable provisions, and one major undesirable provision. In good conscience, I believe that the good outweighs the bad and for that reason, I shall vote for this conference agreement. I support authorizing courts to award a reasonable attorneys' fee to parents who prevail in Public Law 94–142 court actions to enforce their handicapped child's rights and regret that with this conference agreement, we may have made Public Law 94–142's due process hearing system irrevocably litigious and adversarial.

Mr. JEFFORD. Mr. Speaker, I yield myself such time as I may consume.

Mr. Speaker, I rise in support of the conference agreement but I also rise to express my disappointment and concern regarding the outcome of this conference which may be productive. Those who know me, know that I am a staunch supporter of the programs that provide our handicapped children the opportunity and access to free and appropriate education. I am also an advocate of eliminating the barriers that parents may face in trying to assure such an education for their children. One specific barrier is the availability of resources to pay for the services of an attorney. That is what this bill is all about. Should the ability to pay for the services of an attorney determine which students have a better chance of receiving appropriate services and placement because they can afford an attorney to represent them at the various stages of administrative appeal and litigation?

I think we would all agree that the answer to that question is a resounding "no." Clearly, when the participation of an attorney in the process is appropriate, the ability to pay for such services should not determine who gets adequate resolution of their appeals. I believe though, that in addition to providing for reasonable attorneys' fees when parents prevail in court, this conference agreement will encourage the intervention of attorneys at a much earlier stage in the negotiations process.

I was hopeful that we could retain some meaningful oversight regarding the provision of fees at the administrative proceedings level.

For that reason, I was supportive of a provision in the House bill which called for a sunset of the provisions which provided for fees at the administrative level. Unless, after extensive study, there was considerable doubt regarding fees at the administrative level, I am sure that there would have been little difficulty reaffirming our support for such payment. Because we have received such conflicting and diverse information from the field regarding not only the cost, but the effect on the overall process, of providing for fees at the administrative level, I felt that we needed time to carefully review the results of allowing fees at that level. Unfortunately, the sunset provision did not prevail.

Even with these reservations, the benefit of this legislation outweigh its limitations. All children have the right to a free and appropriate education. Parents have the right and responsibility to protect these rights. We must act to retain these rights. I hope that in a few years I will be able to come back to this body and report that my concerns regarding this legislation were unfounded.

I support the provisions of this conference report that address the issues raised by the Supreme Court case, Smith versus Robinson. I do not support the one provision which provides open ended authority to pay attorney's fees at the administrative level. Despite this reservation, I will vote for the conference report and I urge my colleagues to do the same.

Mr. WILLIAMS. Mr. Speaker, I yield back the balance of my time, and I move the previous question on the conference report.

The previous question was ordered.

The conference report was agreed to.

A motion to reconsider was laid on the table.

NOTES

(1) An Addendum on "Whole Code" Considerations

Your review of the preceding pages and work on the problem stated at p. 66 should have given you a view about the likelihood that parents of a child who have successfully challenged a school district's refusal to provide special education for their autistic son can obtain reimbursement for expert witnesses expenses they may have occurred. Had you been working for the GAO at the time, would you have expected your report, called for in Section 4 of the enacted statute, to include information about awards of psychologists' fees? When legislating in the wake of *Alyeska,* Congress had sometimes provided explicitly for the reimbursement of expert witness fees and like expenses, and sometimes had not. These varying statutes had a tendency to come from different committees, and their legislative history neither flagged nor explained the omissions, nor suggested that the proponents of the inclusive statutes thought they were doing anything unusual. For all the indications, the differences were just the product of different drafting styles, different committees, and perhaps the ministrations of different lobbyists.

The following statutory and regulatory texts all existed throughout the period addressed here. How, if at all, do these other elements of federal law, unmentioned in the consideration of the Handicapped Children's Protection Act of 1986 but also treating the question of costs (and substantially reflecting the American rule) affect the conclusion you would reach?

28 U.S.C. § 1821 Per diem and mileage generally; subsistence

(a) (1) Except as otherwise provided by law, a witness in attendance at any court of the United States, or before a United States Magistrate Judge, or before any person authorized to take his deposition pursuant to any rule or order of a court of the United States, shall be paid the fees and allowances provided by this section.

(b) A witness shall be paid an attendance fee of $40 per day for each day's attendance. A witness shall also be paid the attendance fee for the time necessarily occupied in going to and returning from the place of attendance at the beginning and end of such attendance or at any time during such attendance.[3]

[Additional subsections of § 1821 provide for travel costs, subsistence when an overnight stay is required, etc. 28 U.S.C. § 1871 provides at the same rates and in virtually the same terms for *juror* compensation, travel expenses and subsistence if required to live away from home.]

---

[3]   [Ed.] 28 U.S.C. § 1871 provides identically for juror attendance fees.

28 U.S.C. § 1920 Taxation of costs

A judge or clerk of any court of the United States may tax as costs the following:

(1) Fees of the clerk and marshal;

(2) Fees of the court reporter for all or any part of the stenographic transcript necessarily obtained for use in the case;

(3) Fees and disbursements for printing and witnesses;

(4) Fees for exemplification and copies of papers necessarily obtained for use in the case;

(5) Docket fees under section 1923 of this title;

(6) Compensation of court appointed experts, compensation of interpreters, and salaries, fees, expenses, and costs of special interpretation services under section 1828 of this title.

A bill of costs shall be filed in the case and, upon allowance, included in the judgment or decree.

Federal Rules of Civil Procedure Rule 54, Judgments; Costs

. . . (d) Except when express provision therefor is made either in a statute of the United States or in these rules, costs shall be allowed as of course to the prevailing party unless the court otherwise directs.

(2) The Judicial-Congressional Dialogue Continues

One year after Congress enacted the Handicapped Children's Protection Act of 1986, in CRAWFORD FITTING CO. ET AL. V. J. T. GIBBONS, INC., 482 U.S. 437 (1987), the Supreme Court sharply rejected claims for reimbursement of expert witness fees as an element of "costs," relying on the American rule and Section 1821's provision for a daily attendance fee for all witnesses, expert or not. "Any argument that a federal court is empowered to exceed the limitations explicitly set out in §§ 1920 and 1821 without plain evidence of congressional intent to supersede those sections ignores our longstanding practice of construing statutes in pari materia." The prevailing parties claiming the fees were not within any statute providing for the reimbursement of attorneys' fees despite the American rule, and three Justices—Justice Blackmun, concurring, and Justices Marshall and Brennan dissenting—emphasized that the opinion thus did not "reach the question whether, under 42 U.S.C. § 1988, a district court may award fees for an expert witness."

Two years later, in the aftermath of major school desegregation litigation in Kansas City, Missouri, MISSOURI V. JENKINS, 491 U.S. 274 (1989) confirmed the award of market-rate fees for over 15,000 hours work of paralegals and law clerks on the successful plaintiffs' behalf. The Civil Rights Attorney's Fees Awards Act of 1976, 42 U.S.C. § 1988, provided in terms only for "attorneys' fees,"

Clearly, a "reasonable attorney's fee" cannot have been meant to compensate only work performed personally by members of the bar. Rather, the term must refer to a reasonable fee for the work product of an attorney. Thus, the fee must take into account the work not only of attorneys, but also of secretaries, messengers, librarians, janitors, and others whose labor contributes to the work product for which an attorney bills her client; and it must also take account of other expenses and profit. The parties have suggested no reason why the work of paralegals should not be similarly compensated, nor can we think of any. We thus take as our starting point the self-evident proposition that the "reasonable attorney's fee" provided for by statute should compensate the work of paralegals, as well as that of attorneys. . . . Where . . . the prevailing practice is to bill paralegal work at market rates, treating civil rights lawyers' fee requests in the same way is not only permitted by § 1988, but also makes economic sense. By encouraging the use of lower cost paralegals rather than attorneys wherever possible, permitting market-rate billing of paralegal hours "encourages cost-effective delivery of legal services and, by reducing the spiraling cost of civil rights litigation, furthers the policies underlying civil rights statutes." Cameo Convalescent Center, Inc. v. Senn, 738 F.2d 836, 846 (CA7 1984), cert. denied, 469 U.S. 1106 (1985). . . .

Only Chief Justice Rehnquist dissented, arguing "Because law clerks and paralegals have not been licensed to practice law in Missouri, it is difficult to see how charges for their services may be separately billed as part of 'attorney's fees.' . . . I do not think Congress intended the meaning of the statutory term "attorney's fee" to expand and contract with each and every vagary of local billing practice. . . . The language of § 1988 expands the traditional definition of 'costs' to include 'a reasonable attorney's fee,' but it cannot fairly be read to authorize the recovery of all other out-of-pocket expenses actually incurred by the prevailing party in the course of litigation. Absent specific statutory authorization for the recovery of such expenses, the prevailing party remains subject to the limitations on cost recovery imposed by Federal Rule of Civil Procedure 54(d) and 28 U.S.C. § 1920, which govern the taxation of costs in federal litigation where a cost-shifting statute is not applicable."

This reasoning encouraged Judge Posner of the Seventh Circuit to find similar authority in CRAFA for "the judge in a civil rights case [to] order the losing party to reimburse the cost incurred by the winner to hire an expert witness. . . . If 'attorney' in the fee statute can mean something different from attorney, and "fee" something different from fee, then maybe one of the other things "attorney's fee" can mean is the fee paid an expert witness or consultant." Friedrich v. City of Chicago, 888 F.2d 511 (1989). His reasoning was forcefully repudiated, and the stringency of the American rule reasserted in WEST VIRGINIA UNIVERSITY HOSPITALS, INC. V. CASEY, 499 U.S. 83 (1991), substantially relying on the variation in "fee" statutes that sometimes did, but as in the case of

CRAFA often did not, explicitly permit awarding successful plaintiffs expert witness fees. "[The statute's] language is plain and unambiguous. What the Government asks is not a construction of a statute, but, in effect, an enlargement of it by the court, so that what was omitted, presumably by inadvertence, may be included within its scope. To supply omissions transcends the judicial function." Stressing the evident purpose of Congress in enacting CRAFA "to remedy anomalous gaps in our civil rights laws created by . . . Alyeska," Justice Stevens in dissent echoed the dissent in *Smith v. Robinson*," reviewing previous civil rights cases in which Congress had responded "when the Court has put on its thick grammarian's spectacles and ignored the available evidence of congressional purpose and the teaching of prior cases construing a statute . . . [W]e do the country a disservice when we needlessly ignore persuasive evidence of Congress' actual purpose and require it 'to take the time to revisit the matter' and to restate its purpose in more precise English whenever its work product suffers from an omission or inadvertent error."

Congress responded as strongly to *West Virginia University Hospitals* as it had to *Alyeska* and *Smith v. Robinson*. The Civil Rights Act Amendments of 1990 broadly authorized reimbursement of expert witness fees in a civil rights context, but President George H.W. Bush vetoed it. Congress then enacted the Civil Rights Act Amendments of 1991, which he signed into law; its new subsection 1988(c) explicitly provided reimbursement for expert witness expenses "as part of the attorney's fee" for successful litigation under *some, but not all*, of the statutes mentioned in the amended provision:

42 U.S.C. § 1988(b): [The language interpreted in *WVUH*] In any action or proceeding to enforce a provision of sections 1977, 1977A, 1978, 1979, 1980, and 1981 of the Revised Statutes [42 U.S.C.S. §§ 1981–1983], title IX of Public Law 92–318 [20 U.S.C.S. §§ 1681 et seq.], the Religious Freedom Restoration Act of 1993, title VI of the Civil Rights Act of 1964 [42 U.S.C.S. §§ 2000d et seq.], or section 40302 of the Violence Against Women Act of 1994[,] the court, in its discretion, may allow the prevailing party, other than the United States, a reasonable attorney's fee as part of the costs . . .

(c) [New in 1991] In awarding an attorney's fee under subsection (b) in any action or proceeding to enforce a provision of sections 1977 or 1977A of the Revised Statutes [42 U.S.C.S. § 1981], the court, in its discretion, may include expert fees as part of the attorney's fee.

Can you (need you?) imagine reasons for the differentiation that now became part of the law on expert witness fee reimbursement? What are its implications, if any, for the problem of expert witness fees under the Handicapped Children's Protection Act of 1986?

JUDICIAL RESOLUTION

Arlington Central School Dist. Bd. of Education v. Murphy

United States Supreme Court, 2006.
548 U.S. 291.

■ JUSTICE ALITO delivered the opinion of the Court.

Respondents Pearl and Theodore Murphy filed an action under the IDEA[4] on behalf of their son, Joseph Murphy, seeking to require petitioner Arlington Central School District Board of Education to pay for their son's private school tuition for specified school years. Respondents prevailed in the District Court, 86 F.Supp. 2d 354 (SDNY 2000), and the Court of Appeals for the Second Circuit affirmed, 297 F.3d 195 (2002).

As prevailing parents, respondents then sought $29,350 in fees for the services of an educational consultant, Marilyn Arons, who assisted respondents throughout the IDEA proceedings. The District Court granted respondents' request in part. It held that only the value of Arons' time spent between the hearing request and the ruling in respondents' favor could properly be considered charges incurred in an "action or proceeding brought" under the Act. This reduced the maximum recovery to $8,650. The District Court . . . allowed compensation for the full $8,650.

The Court of Appeals for the Second Circuit affirmed. . . . We granted certiorari to resolve the conflict among the Circuits with respect to whether Congress authorized the compensation of expert fees to prevailing parents in IDEA actions. Compare Goldring v. District of Columbia, 416 F.3d 70, 73–77 (CADC 2005); Neosho R-V School Dist. v. Clark ex rel. Clark, 315 F.3d 1022, 1031–1033 (CA8 2003); T. D. v. LaGrange School Dist. No. 102, 349 F.3d 469, 480–482 (CA7 2003). . . .

II

Our resolution of the question presented in this case is guided by the fact that Congress enacted the IDEA pursuant to the Spending Clause. U.S. Const., Art. I, § 8, cl. 1; see Schaffer v. Weast, 546 U.S. 49 (2005). Like its statutory predecessor, the IDEA provides federal funds to assist state and local agencies in educating children with disabilities "and conditions such funding upon a State's compliance with extensive goals and procedures." Board of Ed. of Hendrick Hudson Central School Dist., Westchester Cty. v. Rowley, 458 U.S. 176, 179 (1982).

---

4 [Ed.] The Education of the Handicapped Act (EHA), aka Education of All Handicapped Children Act (EAHCA), became the Individuals with Disabilities Education Act [IDEA] in 1990—the change in title reflecting a wish to stress the individual not a condition. Amendments then and since did not alter the sections with which we are concerned.

Congress has broad power to set the terms on which it disburses federal money to the States, but when Congress attaches conditions to a State's acceptance of federal funds, the conditions must be set out "unambiguously," see Pennhurst State School and Hospital v. Halderman, 451 U.S. 1, 17 (1981); Rowley, supra, at 204, n.26. "[L]egislation enacted pursuant to the spending power is much in the nature of a contract," and therefore, to be bound by "federally imposed conditions," recipients of federal funds must accept them "voluntarily and knowingly." Pennhurst, 451 U.S., at 17. States cannot knowingly accept conditions of which they are "unaware" or which they are "unable to ascertain." Ibid. Thus, in the present case, we must view the IDEA from the perspective of a state official who is engaged in the process of deciding whether the State should accept IDEA funds and the obligations that go with those funds. We must ask whether such a state official would clearly understand that one of the obligations of the Act is the obligation to compensate prevailing parents for expert fees. . . .

III

A

In considering whether the IDEA provides clear notice, we begin with the text. We have "stated time and again that courts must presume that a legislature says in a statute what it means and means in a statute what it says there." Connecticut Nat. Bank v. Germain, 503 U.S. 249, 253–254 (1992). When the statutory "language is plain, the sole function of the courts—at least where the disposition required by the text is not absurd—is to enforce it according to its terms." Hartford Underwriters Ins. Co. v. Union Planters Bank, N.A., 530 U.S. 1, 6 (2000).

The governing provision of the IDEA, 20 U.S.C. § 1415(i)(3)(B), provides that "[i]n any action or proceeding brought under this section, the court, in its discretion, may award reasonable attorneys' fees as part of the costs" to the parents of "a child with a disability" who is the "prevailing party." While this provision provides for an award of "reasonable attorneys' fees," this provision does not even hint that acceptance of IDEA funds makes a State responsible for reimbursing prevailing parents for services rendered by experts.

Respondents contend that we should interpret the term "costs" in accordance with its meaning in ordinary usage and that § 1415(i)(3)(B) should therefore be read to "authorize reimbursement of all costs parents incur in IDEA proceedings, including expert costs."

This argument has multiple flaws. For one thing, as the Court of Appeals in this case acknowledged, " 'costs' is a term of art that generally does not include expert fees." 402 F.3d, at 336. The use of this term of art, rather than a term such as "expenses," strongly suggests that § 1415(i)(3)(B) was not meant to be an open-ended provision that makes participating States liable for all expenses incurred by prevailing parents in connection with an IDEA case—for example, travel and lodging expenses or lost wages due to time taken off from work. Moreover, contrary to respondents' suggestion, § 1415(i)(3)(B) does not say that a court may award "costs" to prevailing parents; rather, it says that a court may award reasonable attorney's fees "as part of the costs" to prevailing parents. This language simply adds reasonable attorney's fees incurred by prevailing parents to the list of costs that prevailing parents are otherwise entitled to recover. This list of otherwise recoverable costs is obviously the list set out in 28 U.S.C. § 1920, the general statute governing the taxation of costs in federal court, and the recovery of witness fees under § 1920 is strictly limited by § 1821, which authorizes travel reimbursement and a $40 per diem. Thus, the text of 20 U.S.C. § 1415(i)(3)(B) does not authorize an award of any additional expert fees, and it certainly fails to provide the clear notice that is required under the Spending Clause.

Other provisions of the IDEA point strongly in the same direction. While authorizing the award of reasonable attorney's fees, the Act contains detailed provisions that are designed to ensure that such awards are indeed reasonable. See §§ 1415(i)(3)(C)–(G). The absence of any comparable provisions relating to expert fees strongly suggests that recovery of expert fees is not authorized. Moreover, the lack of any reference to expert fees in § 1415(d)(2) gives rise to a similar inference. This provision, which generally requires that parents receive "a full explanation of the procedural safeguards" available under § 1415 and refers expressly to "attorneys' fees," makes no mention of expert fees.

B

Respondents contend that their interpretation of § 1415(i)(3)(B) is supported by a provision of the Handicapped Children's Protection Act of 1986 that required the General Accounting Office (GAO) to collect certain data, § 4(b)(3), 100 Stat. 797, but this provision is of little significance for present purposes. The GAO study provision directed the Comptroller General, acting through the GAO, to compile data on, among other things: "(A) the specific amount of attorneys' fees, costs, and expenses awarded to the prevailing party" in IDEA cases for a particular period of time, and (B) "the number of hours spent by personnel, including attorneys and consultants, involved in the action or proceeding, and expenses incurred by the parents and the State educational agency and local educational agency."

Subparagraph (A) would provide some support for respondents' position if it directed the GAO to compile data on awards to prevailing parties of the expense of hiring consultants, but that is not what subparagraph (A) says. Subparagraph (A) makes no mention of consultants or experts or their fees.[1]

---

[1]   Because subparagraph (A) refers to both "costs" and "expenses" awarded to prevailing parties and because it is generally presumed that statutory language is not superfluous, it could be argued that this provision manifests the expectation that prevailing parties would be awarded certain "expenses" not included in the list of "costs" set out in 28 U.S.C. § 1920 and

Subparagraph (B) similarly does not help respondents. Subparagraph (B), which directs the GAO to study "the number of hours spent [in IDEA cases] by personnel, including . . . consultants," says nothing about the award of fees to such consultants. Just because Congress directed the GAO to compile statistics on the hours spent by consultants in IDEA cases, it does not follow that Congress meant for States to compensate prevailing parties for the fees billed by these consultants.

Respondents maintain that "Congress' direction to the GAO would be inexplicable if Congress did not anticipate that the expenses for 'consultants' would be recoverable," but this is incorrect. There are many reasons why Congress might have wanted the GAO to gather data on expenses that were not to be taxed as costs. Knowing the costs incurred by IDEA litigants might be useful in considering future procedural amendments (which might affect these costs) or a future amendment regarding fee shifting. And, in fact, it is apparent that the GAO study provision covered expenses that could not be taxed as costs. For example, the GAO was instructed to compile statistics on the hours spent by all attorneys involved in an IDEA action or proceeding, even though the Act did not provide for the recovery of attorney's fees by a prevailing state or local educational agency.[2] Similarly, the GAO was directed to compile data on "expenses incurred by the parents," not just those parents who prevail and are thus eligible to recover taxed costs.

In sum, the terms of the IDEA overwhelmingly support the conclusion that prevailing parents may not recover the costs of experts or consultants. Certainly the terms of the IDEA fail to provide the clear notice that would be needed to attach such a condition to a State's receipt of IDEA funds.

IV

Thus far, we have considered only the text of the IDEA, but perhaps the strongest support for our interpretation of the IDEA is supplied by our decisions and reasoning in Crawford Fitting Co. v. J.T. Gibbons, Inc., 482 U.S. 437 (1987), and West Virginia University Hospitals, Inc. v. Casey, 499 U.S. 83. In light of those decisions, we do not see how it can be said

---

that expert fees were intended to be among these unenumerated "expenses." This argument fails because, whatever expectation this language might seem to evidence, the fact remains that neither 20 U.S.C. § 1415 nor any other provision of the IDEA authorizes the award of any "expenses" other than "costs." Recognizing this, respondents argue not that they are entitled to recover "expenses" that are not "costs," but that expert fees are recoverable "costs." As a result, the reference to awards of both "expenses" and "costs" does not support respondents' position. The reference to "expenses" may relate to IDEA actions brought in state court, § 1415(i)(2)(A), where "expenses" other than "costs" might be receivable. Or the reference may be surplusage. While it is generally presumed that statutes do not contain surplusage, instances of surplusage are not unknown.

[2] In 2000, the attorneys' fees provision provided only an award to prevailing parents. In 2004, Congress amended § 1415(i)(3)(B) to include . . . awards "to a prevailing party who is a State educational agency or local educational agency" where the complaint filed is frivolous or presented for an improper purpose, such as to harass, delay, or increase the cost of litigation.

that the IDEA gives a State unambiguous notice regarding liability for expert fees. . . .

The reasoning of Crawford Fitting strongly supports the conclusion that the term "costs" in 20 U.S.C. § 1415(i)(3)(B), like the same term in Rule 54(d), is defined by the categories of expenses enumerated in 28 U.S.C. § 1920. This conclusion is buttressed by the principle, recognized in Crawford Fitting, that no statute will be construed as authorizing the taxation of witness fees as costs unless the statute "refer[s] explicitly to witness fees."

Our decision in Casey confirms even more dramatically that the IDEA does not authorize an award of expert fees. . . . The Court of Appeals . . . was heavily influenced by a Casey footnote, but the court misunderstood the footnote's meaning. The text accompanying the footnote argued, based on an analysis of several fee-shifting statutes, that the term "attorney's fees" does not include expert fees. In the footnote, we commented on petitioners' invocation of the Conference Committee Report relating to 20 U.S.C. § 1415(i)(3)(B), which stated: " 'The conferees intend[ed] that the term "attorneys' fees as part of the costs" include reasonable expenses and fees of expert witnesses and the reasonable costs of any test or evaluation which is found to be necessary for the preparation of the . . . case.' " 499 U.S., at 91–92, n.5 (quoting H.R. Conf. Rep. No. 99–687, at 5; ellipsis in original). This statement, the footnote commented, was "an apparent effort to *depart* from ordinary meaning and to define a term of art." 499 U.S., at 92, n.5. The footnote did not state that the Conference Committee Report set out the correct interpretation of § 1415(i)(3)(B), much less that the Report was sufficient, despite the language of the statute, to provide the clear notice required under the Spending Clause. The thrust of the footnote was simply that the term "attorneys' fees," standing alone, is generally not understood as encompassing expert fees. . . .

V

Respondents make several arguments that are not based on the text of the IDEA, but these arguments do not show that the IDEA provides clear notice regarding the award of expert fees.

Respondents argue that their interpretation of the IDEA furthers the Act's overarching goal of "ensur[ing] that all children with disabilities have available to them a free appropriate public education," 20 U.S.C. § 1400(d)(1)(A) as well as the goal of "safeguard[ing] the rights of parents to challenge school decisions that adversely affect their child." Brief for Respondents 20. . . . Because the IDEA is not intended in all instances to further the broad goals identified by the respondents at the expense of fiscal considerations, the goals cited by respondents do little to bolster their argument on the narrow question presented here.[3]

---

[3] Respondents note that a GAO report stated that expert witness fees are reimbursable expenses. See Brief for Respondents 19 (citing GAO, Special Education: The Attorney Fees

Finally, respondents vigorously argue that Congress clearly intended for prevailing parents to be compensated for expert fees. They rely on the legislative history of § 1415 and in particular on the following statement in the Conference Committee Report, discussed above: "The conferees intend that the term 'attorneys' fees as part of the costs' include reasonable expenses and fees of expert witnesses and the reasonable costs of any test or evaluation which is found to be necessary for the preparation of the . . . case." H.R. Conf. Rep. No. 99–687, at 5.

Whatever weight this legislative history would merit in another context, it is not sufficient here. Putting the legislative history aside, we see virtually no support for respondents' position. Under these circumstances, where everything other than the legislative history overwhelming suggests that expert fees may not be recovered, the legislative history is simply not enough. In a Spending Clause case, the key is not what a majority of the Members of both Houses intend but what the States are clearly told regarding the conditions that go along with the acceptance of those funds. Here, in the face of the unambiguous text of the IDEA and the reasoning in Crawford Fitting and Casey, we cannot say that the legislative history on which respondents rely is sufficient to provide the requisite fair notice.

* * *

We reverse the judgment of the Court of Appeals for the Second Circuit and remand the case for further proceedings consistent with this opinion.

It is so ordered.

■ JUSTICE GINSBURG, concurring in part and concurring in the judgment.

I agree, in the main, with the Court's resolution of this case, but part ways with the Court's . . . "clear notice" requirement [for measures . . . enacted] . . . pursuant to the Spending Clause. . . . [In Pennhurst, the Court] confronted a plea to impose "an unexpected condition for compliance—a new [programmatic] obligation for participating States." Bell v. New Jersey, 461 U.S. 773, 790, n. 17 (1983). The controversy here is lower key: It concerns not the educational programs IDEA directs school districts to provide, but "the remedies available against a noncomplying [district]." Ibid.

. . . IDEA was enacted not only pursuant to Congress' Spending Clause authority, but also pursuant to § 5 of the Fourteenth Amendment. . . . Furthermore, no "clear notice" prop is needed in this case given the twin pillars on which the Court's judgment securely rests. First, as the Court explains, the specific, attorneys'-fees-oriented, provisions of IDEA "overwhelmingly support the conclusion that prevailing parents may not recover the costs of experts or consultants."

Provision of Public Law 99–372, p. 13 (Nov. 1989)). But this passing reference in a report issued by an agency not responsible for implementing the IDEA is plainly insufficient to provide clear notice regarding the scope of the conditions attached to the receipt of IDEA funds.

... Second, as the Court develops, prior decisions closely in point "strongly suppor[t]," even "confir[m] ... dramatically," today's holding that IDEA trains on attorneys' fees and does not authorize an award covering amounts paid or payable for the services of an educational consultant. ... Given the constant meaning of the formulation "attorneys' fees as part of the costs" in federal legislation, we are not at liberty to rewrite "the statutory text adopted by both Houses of Congress and submitted to the President," to add several words Congress wisely might have included. The ball, I conclude, is properly left in Congress' court to provide, if it so elects, for consultant fees and testing expenses beyond those IDEA and its implementing regulations already authorize,[4] along with any specifications, conditions, or limitations geared to those fees and expenses Congress may deem appropriate. Cf. § 1415(i)(3)(B)–(G); § 1415(d)(2)(L) (listing only attorneys' fees, not expert or consulting fees, among the procedural safeguards about which school districts must inform parents).

■ JUSTICE SOUTER, dissenting [omitted].

■ JUSTICE BREYER, with whom JUSTICE STEVENS and JUSTICE SOUTER join, dissenting.

The Individuals with Disabilities Education Act (IDEA or Act),[3] 20 U.S.C.A. § 1400 *et seq.*, (Supp. 2006), says that a court may "award reasonable attorneys' fees as part of the costs to the parents" who are prevailing parties. § 1415(i)(3)(B). Unlike the Court, I believe that the word "costs" includes, and authorizes payment of, the costs of experts. The word "costs" does not define its own scope. Neither does the phrase "attorneys' fees as part of costs." But Members of Congress did make clear their intent by, among other things, approving a Conference Report that specified that "the term 'attorneys' fees as part of the costs' include[s] reasonable expenses of expert witnesses and reasonable costs of any test or evaluation which is found to be necessary for the preparation of the parent or guardian's case in the action or proceeding." H.R. Conf. Rep. No. 99–687, p. 5 (1986). No Senator or Representative voiced *any* opposition to this statement in the discussion preceding the vote on the Conference Report—the last vote on the bill before it was sent to the President. I can find no good reason for this Court to interpret the language of this statute as meaning the precise opposite of what Congress told us it intended.

I

There are two strong reasons for interpreting the statutory phrase to include the award of expert fees. First, that is what Congress said it

----

[4] Under 34 C.F.R. § 300.502(b)(1) (2005), a "parent has the right to an independent educational evaluation at public expense if the parent disagrees with an evaluation obtained by the public agency."

[3] See n. 1, p. 127 above.

intended by the phrase. Second, that interpretation furthers the IDEA's statutorily defined purposes.

A

Congress added the IDEA's cost-shifting provision when it enacted the Handicapped Children's Protection Act of 1986 (HCPA), 100 Stat. 796. Senator Lowell Weicker introduced the relevant bill in 1985. 131 Cong. Rec. 1979–1980 (1985). As introduced, it sought to overturn this Court's determination that the then-current version of the IDEA (and other civil rights statutes) did not authorize courts to award attorneys' fees to prevailing parents in IDEA cases. See Smith v. Robinson, 468 U.S. 992 (1984). The bill provided that "[i]n any action or proceeding brought under this subsection, the court, in its discretion, may award a reasonable attorney's fee as part of the costs to a parent or legal representative of a handicapped child or youth who is the prevailing party." 131 Cong. Rec. 1980; see S.Rep. No. 99–112, p.2 (1985).

After hearings and debate, several Senators introduced a new bill in the Senate that would have put a cap on attorneys' fees for legal services lawyers, but at the same time would have explicitly authorized the award of "a reasonable attorney's fee, reasonable witness fees, and *other reasonable expenses of the civil action*, in addition to the costs to a parent . . . who is the prevailing party." Id., at 7 (emphasis added). While no Senator objected to the latter provision, some objected to the cap. (Additional Views of Senators Kerry, Kennedy, Pell, Dodd, Simon, Metzenbaum and Matsunaga) A bipartisan group of Senators, led by Senators Hatch and Weicker, proposed an alternative bill that authorized courts to award "a reasonable attorney's fee in addition to the costs to a parent" who prevailed.

Senator Weicker explained that the bill:

"will enable courts to compensate parents for *whatever reasonable costs they had to incur to fully secure what was guaranteed to them by the EHA*. As in other fee shifting statutes, it is our intent that such awards will include, at the discretion of the court, reasonable attorney's fees, *necessary expert witness fees, and other reasonable expenses which were necessary for parents to vindicate their claim to a free appropriate public education for their handicapped child*." 131 Cong. Rec. at 21390 (emphasis added).

Not a word of opposition to this statement (or the provision) was voiced on the Senate floor, and S. 415 passed without a recorded vote.

The House version of the bill also reflected an intention to authorize recovery of expert costs. Following the House hearings, the Committee on Education and Labor produced a substitute bill that authorized courts to "award reasonable attorneys' fees, *expenses and costs*" to prevailing parents. H.R. Rep. No. 99–296, pp.1, 5 (1985) (emphasis added). The House Report stated that

"The phrase 'expenses and costs' includes *expenses of expert witnesses; the reasonable costs of any study, report, test, or project which is found to be necessary for the preparation of the parents' or guardian's due process hearing, state administrative review or civil action;* as well as traditional costs and expenses incurred in the course of litigating a case (e.g., depositions and interrogatories)." Id., at 6 (emphasis added).

No one objected to this statement. By the time H.R. 1523 reached the floor, another substitute bill was introduced. 131 Cong. Rec. 31369 (1985). This new bill did not change in any respect the text of the authorization of expenses and costs. It did add a provision, however, that directed the General Accounting Office (GAO)—now known as the Government Accountability Office, see 31 U.S.C.A. § 731 note (Supp. 2006)—to study and report to Congress on the fiscal impact of the cost-shifting provision. The newly substituted bill passed the House without a recorded vote.

Members of the House and Senate (including all of the primary sponsors of the HCPA) then met in conference to work out certain differences. At the conclusion of those negotiations, they produced a Conference Report, which contained the text of the agreed-upon bill and a "Joint Explanatory Statement of the Committee of the Conference." [Justice Breyer appended the Conference Report to his opinion.] The Conference accepted the House bill's GAO provision with "an amendment expanding the data collection requirements of the GAO study to include information regarding the amount of funds expended by local educational agencies and state educational agencies on civil actions and administrative proceedings." And it accepted (with minor changes) the cost-shifting provisions provided in both the Senate and House versions. The conferees explained:

"With slightly different wording, both the Senate bill and the House amendment provide for the awarding of attorneys' fees in addition to costs. The Senate recedes to the House and the House recedes to the Senate with an amendment clarifying that 'the court, in its discretion, may award reasonable attorneys' fees as part of the costs . . . ' This change in wording incorporates the Supreme Court['s] Marek v. Chesny decision [473 U.S 1 (1985)]. *The conferees intend that the term 'attorneys' fees as part of the costs' include reasonable expenses and fees of expert witnesses and the reasonable costs of any test or evaluation which is found to be necessary for the preparation of the parent or guardian's case in the action or proceeding, as well as traditional costs incurred in the course of litigating a case." Id.,* at 5 (emphasis added; citation omitted).

The Conference Report was returned to the Senate and the House. A motion was put to each to adopt the Conference Report, and both the Senate and the House agreed to the Conference Report by voice votes. See Appendix B, infra, (Senate); Appendix C, infra (House). No objection was raised to the Conference Report's statement that the cost-shifting provision was intended to authorize expert costs. I concede that "sponsors of the legislation did not mention anything on the floor about expert or consultant fees" at the time the Conference Report was submitted. But . . . *every* Senator and *three of the five* Representatives who spoke on the floor had previously *signed his name* to the Conference Report—a Report that made Congress' intent clear on the first page of its explanation. And every Senator and Representative that took the floor preceding the votes voiced his strong support for the Conference Report. The upshot is that Members of both Houses of Congress voted to adopt both the statutory text before us and the Conference Report that made clear that the statute's words include the expert costs here in question.

B

The Act's basic purpose further supports interpreting the provision's language to include expert costs. The IDEA guarantees a "free" and "appropriate" public education for "all" children with disabilities. 20 U.S.C.A. § 1400(d)(1)(A) (Supp. 2006). . . . § 1400(c)(5)(B) (IDEA "ensur[es] that families of [disabled] children have meaningful opportunities to participate in the education of their children at school"). . . . And in doing so, they may secure the help of experts. § 1415(h)(1). . . . The practical significance of the Act's participatory rights and procedural protections may be seriously diminished if parents are unable to obtain reimbursement for the costs of their experts. In IDEA cases, experts are necessary. [Citing studies and a dissenting opinion by Justice Ginsburg.]

Experts are also expensive. The costs of experts may not make much of a dent in a school district's budget, as many of the experts they use in IDEA proceedings are already on the staff. But to parents, the award of costs may matter enormously. Without potential reimbursement, parents may well lack the services of experts entirely. [Citing studies suggesting a strong connection between disability and limited parental economic resources. E.g., 65% of disabled children live in households with incomes less than $50,000][5]

In a word, the Act's statutory right to a "free" and "appropriate" education may mean little to those who must pay hundreds of dollars to obtain it. That is why this Court has previously avoided interpretations that would bring about this kind of result. See School Comm. of Burlington v. Department of Ed. of Mass., 471 U.S. 359 (1985); Florence County School Dist. Four v. Carter, 510 U.S. 7, 13 (1993). In Carter, we explained: "IDEA was intended to ensure that children with disabilities receive an education that is both appropriate and free. To read the provisions of § 1401(a)(18) to bar reimbursement in the circumstances of

---

[5]   [Ed.] Respondents' brief remarked that the Murphys' income fit this parameter, and that they had conducted the litigation without an attorney through the eight proceedings preceding the Supreme Court's consideration. The editor of these materials was a signatory of that brief, having been invited to join the litigation after the prior publication of the first edition of this book.

this case would defeat this statutory purpose." *Id.*, at 13–14 (citation omitted). . . .

To read the word "costs" as requiring successful parents to bear their own expenses for experts suffers from the same problem. Today's result will leave many parents and guardians "without an expert with the firepower to match the opposition," Schaffer [v. Weast], (slip op., at 11), a far cry from the level playing field that Congress envisioned.

II

The majority makes essentially three arguments against this interpretation. It says that the statute's purpose and "legislative history is simply not enough" to overcome: (1) the fact that this is a Spending Clause case; (2) the text of the statute; and (3) our prior cases which hold that the term "costs" does not include expert costs. I do not find these arguments convincing.

A

At the outset the majority says that it "is guided by the fact that Congress enacted the IDEA pursuant to the Spending Clause." . . . I agree that the statute on its face does not *clearly* tell the States that they must pay expert fees to prevailing parents. But I do not agree that the majority has posed the right question. For one thing, we have repeatedly examined the nature and extent of the financial burdens that the IDEA imposes without reference to the Spending Clause or any "clear-statement rule." [citing cases.]

For another thing, neither Pennhurst nor any other case suggests that *every spending detail* of a Spending Clause statute must be spelled out with unusual clarity. . . . [A]mbiguity about the precise nature of a statutory program's details—particularly where they are of a kind that States might have anticipated—is rarely relevant to the basic question: Would the States have accepted the Federal Government's funds *had they only known* the nature of the accompanying conditions? . . . Given the nature of such details, it is [usually] clear that the States would have entered the program regardless. At the same time, to view each statutory detail of a highly complex federal/state program (involving say, transportation, schools, the environment) simply through the lens of linguistic clarity, rather than to assess its meanings in terms of basic legislative purpose, is to risk a set of judicial interpretations that can prevent the program, overall, from achieving its basic objectives or that might well reduce a program in its details to incoherence.

This case is about just such a detail. Permitting parents to recover expert fees will not lead to awards of "indeterminate magnitude, untethered to compensable harm" and consequently will not "pose a concern that recipients of federal funding could not reasonably have anticipated." Barnes, 536 U.S., at 191 (SOUTER, J., joined by O'CONNOR, J., concurring). . . .

B

If the Court believes that the statute's language is unambiguous, I must disagree. The provision at issue says that a court "may award reasonable attorneys' fees as part of the costs" to parents who prevail in an action brought under the Act. The statute neither defines the word "costs" nor points to any other source of law for a definition. And the word "costs," alone, says nothing at all about which costs falls within its scope.

Neither does the statutory phrase—"as part of the costs to the parents of a child with a disability who is the prevailing party"—taken in its entirety unambiguously foreclose an award of expert fees. I agree that, read literally, that provision does not clearly grant authority to award any costs at all. And one might read it, as the Court does, as referencing another federal statute, 28 U.S.C. § 1920, which provides that authority. But such a reading is not inevitable. The provision (indeed, the entire Act) says nothing about that other statute. And one can, consistent with the language, read the provision as both embodying a general authority to award costs while also specifying the inclusion of "reasonable attorneys' fees" as part of those costs (as saying, for example, that a court "may award reasonable attorneys' fees as part of [a] costs [award]").

This latter reading, while linguistically the less natural, is legislatively the more likely. The majority's alternative reading, by cross-referencing only the federal general cost-awarding statute (which applies solely *in federal courts*), would produce a jumble of different cost definitions applicable to similar IDEA administrative and state-court proceedings in different States. This result is particularly odd, as all IDEA actions must begin in state due process hearings, where the federal cost statute clearly does not apply, and the overwhelming majority of these actions are never appealed to *any* court. And when parents do appeal, they can file their actions in either state or federal courts. 20 U.S.C.A. § 1415(i)(2)(A) (Supp. 2006).

Would Congress "obviously" have wanted the content of the word "costs" to vary from State to State, proceeding to proceeding? Why? At most, the majority's reading of the text is plausible; it is not the only possible reading.

C

The majority's most persuasive argument does not focus on either the Spending Clause or lack of statutory ambiguity. Rather, the majority says that "costs" is a term of art. In light of the law's long practice of excluding expert fees from the scope of the word "costs," along with this Court's cases interpreting the word similarly in other statutes, the "legislative history is simply not enough."

I am perfectly willing to assume that the majority is correct about the traditional scope of the word "costs." . . . But Congress is free to redefine terms of art. . . . [And] here the statute itself indicates that

Congress did not intend to use the word "costs" as a term of art. The HCPA, which added the cost-shifting provision (in § 2) to the IDEA, also added another provision (in § 4) directing the GAO to "conduct a study of the impact of the amendments to the [IDEA] made by section 2" over a 312 year period following the Act's effective date. § 4(a), 100 Stat. 797. To determine the fiscal impact of § 2 (the cost-shifting provision), § 4 ordered the GAO to submit a report to Congress containing, among other things, the following information:

> "Data, for a geographically representative select sample of States, indicating (A) *the specific amount of attorneys' fees, costs, and expenses awarded to the prevailing party*, in each action and proceeding under [§ 2] from the date of the enactment of this Act through fiscal year 1988, *and* the range of such *fees, costs and expenses* awarded in the actions and proceedings under such section, categorized by type of complaint and (B) for the same sample as in (A) *the number of hours spent by personnel, including attorneys and consultants*, involved in the action or proceeding, and expenses incurred by the parents and the State educational agency and local educational agency." § 4(b)(3), *id.,* at 797–798 (emphasis added).

If Congress intended the word "costs" in § 2 to authorize an award of only those costs listed in the federal cost statute, why did it use the word "expenses" in § 4(b)(3)(A) as part of the "amount awarded to the prevailing party"? When used as a term of art, after all, "costs" does not cover expenses. Nor does the federal costs statute cover any expenses— at least not any that Congress could have wanted the GAO to study.

Further, why did Congress, when asking the GAO (in the statute itself) to study the "numbers of hours spent by personnel" include among those personnel both attorneys *"and consultants"*? Who but experts could those consultants be? Why would Congress want the GAO to study the hours that those experts "spent," unless it thought that it would help keep track of the "costs" that the statute imposed?

Of course, one might, through speculation, find other answers to these questions. . . . But these answers are not necessarily consistent with the purpose of the GAO study provision, a purpose revealed by the language of the provision and its position in the statute. Its placement and its reference to § 2 indicate that Congress ordered the study to help it keep track of the magnitude of the reimbursements that an earlier part of the new statute (namely, § 2) mandated. See 100 Stat. 797 (stating that purpose of GAO study was to determine the "impact" of "section 2"). And the *only* reimbursement requirement that § 2 mandates is the payment of "costs."

But why speculate about this? We *know* what Congress intended the GAO study to cover. It *told* the GAO in its Conference Report that the word "costs" included the costs of experts. And, not surprisingly, the GAO made clear that it understood precisely what Congress asked it to do. In its final report, the GAO wrote: "Parents can receive reimbursement from state or local education agencies for some or all of their attorney fees *and related expenses* if they are the prevailing party in part or all of administrative hearings or court proceedings. *Expert witness fees, costs of tests or evaluations found to be necessary during the case, and court costs for services rendered during administrative and court proceedings are examples of reimbursable expenses.*" GAO, Briefing Report to Congressional Requesters, Special Education: The Attorney Fees Provision of Public Law 99–372 GAO/HRD-22BR, p. 13 (Nov. 1989). At the very least, this amounts to *some* indication that Congress intended the word "costs," not as a term of art, not as it was used in the statutes at issue in Casey and Crawford Fitting, but rather as including certain additional "expenses." If that is so, the claims of tradition, of the interpretation this Court has given other statutes, cannot be so strong as to prevent us from examining the legislative history. And that history could not be more clear about the matter: Congress intended the statutory phrase "attorneys' fees as part of the costs" to include the costs of experts. See Part I, supra.

III

For the reasons I have set forth, I cannot agree with the majority's conclusion. Even less can I agree with its failure to consider fully the statute's legislative history. That history makes Congress' purpose clear. And our ultimate judicial goal is to interpret language in light of the statute's purpose. Only by seeking that purpose can we avoid the substitution of judicial for legislative will. Only by reading language in its light can we maintain the democratic link between voters, legislators, statutes, and ultimate implementation, upon which the legitimacy of our constitutional system rests.

In my view, to keep faith with that interpretive goal, we must retain all traditional interpretive tools—text, structure, history, and purpose. And, because faithful interpretation is art as well as science, we cannot, through rule or canon, rule out the use of any of these tools, automatically and in advance.

Nothing in the Constitution forbids us from giving significant weight to legislative history. By disregarding a clear statement in a legislative report adopted without opposition in both Houses of Congress, the majority has reached a result no Member of Congress expected or overtly desired. It has adopted an interpretation that undercuts, rather than furthers, the statute's purpose, a "free" and "appropriate" public education for "all" children with disabilities. And it has adopted an approach that, I fear, divorces law from life.

For these reasons, I respectfully dissent.

NOTES ON MURPHY

(1) Consider the methodologies, and also the tone, of these opinions for the Court in June, 2006. If you were now arguing a case about statutory interpretation to this Court, what tack would you take?

Does there appear to be any disagreement among the Justices that interpretation (and therefore lawyers' arguments) must begin with the text at issue? How important, then, is it for you as a lawyer to begin by persuading the Court that the text of the statutory language at issue leaves room for the interpretation you wish to support—that its text *could* mean what you contend it *does* mean? What kinds of arguments and materials appear to be persuasive in that task? And if you do succeed in persuading the Court that the statute has room for the meaning you support, but must recognize that other readings of that text are also possible, what techniques appear to be effective for getting the Justices from *could* mean to *does* mean? Is use of legislative materials foreclosed? If you do use such materials in arguing the case, would it be advisable to address such issues as reliability, as well as the content of the materials as such?

(2) Justices made the following statements during the *Murphy* oral argument:[6]

> Mr. Kuntz (for the School Board): [The Conference Report language about reimbursement of expert witnesses] emanates solely from the House conference report.
>
> **Justice Scalia:**—Well, that's only half of the Congress, isn't it? . . . So we have a committee of one house . . . that thought it meant that or would have liked it to mean that.
>
> Mr. Kuntz: Yes, Your Honor. . . .
>
> **Justice Stevens:** How do you explain the title, Joint Explanatory Statement of the Committee of the Conference? Doesn't that speak for both the House and the Senate?
>
> Mr. Kuntz: It . . . yes, Your Honor, it does.
>
> **Chief Justice Roberts:** Counsel, sometimes these joint statements are actually voted on by the Congress as a whole. Was this one voted on?
>
> Mr. Kuntz: There was no evidence of that, Your Honor, in our review. . . .
>
> **Justice Scalia:** They are voted on . . . when the conferees make changes, which they sometimes do. Then . . . of course, they have to be voted on. So it's . . . frequent that they're voted on, but this one apparently . . . there were no changes made and it wasn't voted on. [sic]

---

6   http://www.oyez.org/cases/2000–2009/2005/2005_05_18#argument.

Mr. Vladeck (for the Murphys): . . . So I think that at least in the conference report, Congress is signaling that if there were other costs that were incurred unreasonably as a result of lawyers protracting or delaying a proceeding, they too would be subject to the same reduction.

Justice Scalia: And that's effective too, as though it were written into the statute, because one committee of Congress said so. . . .

Mr. Vladeck: Well, Your Honor, this is not one committee of Congress. This was . . . the conference report was circulated to all Members of Congress before they voted on the final bill.

Justice Scalia: And . . . and they read it.

Mr. Vladeck: Well, Your Honor, this is the final bill they voted on, and if they turned the page—

Justice Scalia: That's the only thing we know for sure that they voted on.

Mr. Vladeck:—. . . The vote was a vote to approve the conference report, which contains . . . three pages of text and three pages of explanation.

Might the Justices' evident failures to understand the conference report process have influenced the outcome? How might they be remedied? Or are these interchanges just evidence of immovable views?

(3) The opinions in *Murphy* contest the meaning of Section 4 of the Act, calling for a GAO report that could readily have been taken (and by the GAO *was* taken) to assume that expert witness fees could be reimbursed. This is a classic example of "whole act" argumentation— questioning whether the ordinary rather than the law-inflected term of art meaning could be ascribed to "costs"—an argument that also seems supported by the whole phrase "costs to the parents"; it is hardly necessary to refer to parental costs if one means to provide only for the awarding of conventional court costs. The GAO report provision had not figured in *any* of the judicial opinions favoring parental recovery that preceded the Supreme Court argument in *Murphy*. It was in fact found, and its possible significance first appreciated, by a student studying these materials at an earlier point in their development. In considering the whole act in your own work on the problem, did you find it?

Other possible "whole act" arguments were not found until *after* briefing and argument in *Murphy*—some by other students and another while preparing these materials. Hopefully it will have become apparent just how important—and difficult—attention to "whole act" possibilities can be. And this statute was relatively brief, and the product of single committees in each House that showed signs of having given its text careful consideration. Did you find these possible arguments?

20 U.S.C. § 1415—Procedural safeguards . . .

(i) Administrative procedures . . .

(3) Jurisdiction of district courts; attorneys' fees

(D) Prohibition of attorneys' fees and related costs for certain services

(i) In general Attorneys' fees may not be awarded and related costs may not be reimbursed in any action or proceeding under this section for services performed subsequent to the time of a written offer of settlement to a parent if—

(I) the offer is made within the time prescribed by Rule 68 of the Federal Rules of Civil Procedure or, in the case of an administrative proceeding, at any time more than 10 days before the proceeding begins;

(II) the offer is not accepted within 10 days; and

(III) the court or administrative hearing officer finds that the relief finally obtained by the parents is not more favorable to the parents than the offer of settlement. . . .

(E) Exception to prohibition on attorneys' fees and related costs

Notwithstanding subparagraph (D), an award of attorneys' fees and related costs may be made to a parent who is the prevailing party and who was substantially justified in rejecting the settlement offer. [Emphases added]

Might it have made a difference if the Murphys' attorneys had argued that the repeated references to "related costs," which might be "reimbursed," signaled that the enacting Congress understood "costs" in its ordinary meaning, rather than as a reference to the American rule and 28 U.S.C.? "Related costs" are not defined in the statute, but the statute does define "related services" in a way that clearly includes psychological assessments. 20 U.S.C. § 1401(26)(A). Or were the majority Justices simply immovable in normatively-grounded resistance to the reimbursement of expert witness fees?

20 U.S.C. § 1411—Authorization; allotment; use of funds; authorization of appropriations . . .

(e) State level Activities . . .

(3) Local educational agency risk pool . . .

(E) Legal fees

The disbursements [from the high-cost fund] shall not support legal fees, *court costs, or other costs* associated with a cause of action brought on behalf of a child with a disability to ensure a free appropriate public education for such child. [Emphasis added]

There's a moral here:

Read the statute, *Read the Statute*, **READ THE STATUTE!!!**